FINDING GOD
IN THE
QUESTIONS

DR. TIMOTHY
JOHNSON

InterVarsity Press
Downers Grove, Illinois

InterVarsity Press
P.O. Box 1400, Downers Grove, IL 60515-1426
World Wide Web: www.ivpress.com
E-mail: mail@ivpress.com

InterVarsity Press® is the book-publishing division of InterVarsity Christian Fellowship/USA®, a student
movement active on campus at hundreds of universities, colleges and schools of nursing in the United States
of America, and a member movement of the International Fellowship of Evangelical Students. For
information about local and regional activities, write Public Relations Dept., InterVarsity Christian
Fellowship/USA, 6400 Schroeder Rd., P.O. Box 7895, Madison, WI 53707-7895, or visit the IVCF website
at <www.intervarsity.org>.

All Scripture quotations, unless otherwise indicated, are taken from the Good News Bible, Second Edition,
Today's English Version, Copyright ©1992 by American Bible Society. Used by permission. All rights reserved.

Every effort has been made to provide proper credit for material cited in this book. Omissions and errors
should be brought to the attention of the publisher for correction in future editions.

Design: Cindy Kiple

Images: Molly Lynch/ABC Photography Archives

ISBN 0-8308-3214-9

Printed in the United States of America ∞

Library of Congress Cataloging-in-Publication Data

Johnson, G. Timothy, 1936-
    Finding God in the questions: a personal journey / Timothy Johnson.
        p. cm.
    Includes bibliographical references.
    ISBN 0-8308-3214-9 (alk. paper)
    1. Apologetics. 2. Religion and science. 3. Christian life. 4.
    Johnson, G. Timothy, 1936- I. Title.
BT1103.J64 2004
230—dc22

                                                                                        2003027940

| P | 19 | 18 | 17 | 16 | 15 | 14 | 13 | 12 | 11 | 10 | 9 | 8 | 7 | 6 | 5 | 4 | 3 | 2 | 1 |
| Y | 18 | 17 | 16 | 15 | 14 | 13 | 12 | 11 | 10 | 09 | 08 | 07 | 06 | 05 | 04 | | | | |

To my late parents,

Eunice and Henning Johnson.

Their own commitment to following Jesus

still inspires me to attempt the same.

CONTENTS

PREFACE

❧

In a sense, writing this book has been an attempt to be totally honest about my religious beliefs for the first time in forty years. I graduated from seminary forty years ago; and ever since, I have been able to avoid facing the full consequences of what I truly believe—and what I can't believe. Since I never became a full-time minister to a congregation but instead went to medical school and became a physician, I never had to examine what I believed thoroughly enough to allow me to be a person of spiritual integrity day in and day out. In other words, I was able to have it both ways: I could believe what was comfortable and useful in my mostly secular life without having to test it in the fires of real spiritual struggle to determine what I actually believed—and what that belief required of me in the choices of my daily life.

Not that I tried to hide the fact that I was a clergyman. Indeed, it is well known to most of my colleagues in medicine and media that I am a believer and a minister. That's why they have often come to me for spiritual as well as medical advice—and why I am often asked to perform weddings for friends and colleagues. I never tried to hide this part of my background—but I never had to take full responsibility for how my beliefs should shape my everyday life. And I have always been able to move easily between my secular and spiritual lives without having to completely blend them in a manner that would cause me any pain or sacrifice.

With the writing of this book, that will no longer be possible. I am now compelled to face my beliefs with candor and confession. The task both frightens and excites me. I know some who admire my secular achievements will be turned off by this spiritual exploration—and some who admire my spiritual stance will be disappointed in my conclusions. At this point in my life, I am finally willing to take those chances. As the saying goes, better late than never.

Here's to asking questions.

ACKNOWLEDGMENTS

B elief is ultimately a matter of individual choice, but exploring questions of faith is best done in community. I have been inspired by reading the insights and struggles of other seekers, whether they are formally religious or not. At the end of this book you will find some suggestions for further reading to acquaint you with other points of view if you wish to pursue them.

Throughout the writing of this book, I have also been greatly helped by the comments and criticisms of many friends and colleagues (from the worlds of science, media and theology) who were willing to take the time to read my manuscript and offer honest (sometimes brutally so) feedback. I have decided not to list their many names lest I forget some or include some who may not wish to be so identified. They all know how much they have helped me shape my thoughts and therefore this book. There are, however, three people I must thank specifically.

Bob Fryling, the publisher of InterVarsity Press, called me one morning at my office to say that he had been given my manuscript by a mutual friend (a surprise to me!) and was very interested in publishing it. That was good enough for me. My whole life has unfolded in unexpected and unplanned ways (I have never had an agent for TV work), and I view such calls or contacts as gifts from God. Throughout this project, Bob has been a faithful supporter.

After I had completed a first draft, another friend suggested I get in touch with Kathy Helmers, who operates her own literary agency in Colorado Springs. She also responded with enthusiasm and greatly helped me further shape and reorganize my thinking. She has been a constant companion in this project, and I greatly value her input and friendship. I also wish to thank Al Hsu, who has been my editor during the final stages of this book. Al is my kind of co-worker: brisk, honest and to the point. I have trusted his input and judgments completely.

Finally, I wish to thank my wife, Nancy, who has patiently endured my frantic efforts to find the time to finish this book. She has made my life at home so easy that I fear I take it for granted. I hope when she reads this she will realize how much I appreciate her loving care.

P.S. I am in awe of charitable organizations serving the poor and disadvantaged. All profits to me from the publication of this book will be donated to such groups.

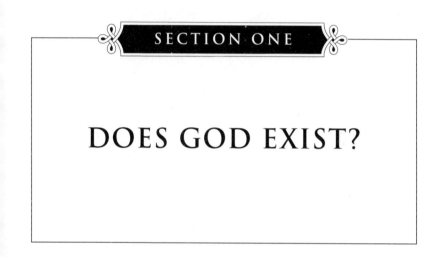

SECTION ONE

DOES GOD EXIST?

1

WHY DO THE QUESTIONS KEEP COMING?

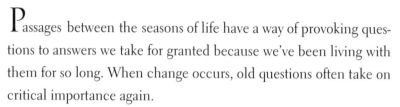

Passages between the seasons of life have a way of provoking questions to answers we take for granted because we've been living with them for so long. When change occurs, old questions often take on critical importance again.

For many people religion provides answers (or at least a sense of security) to the big questions of life. For others the absolute claims of religion raise more questions than they answer. I have lived on both sides—and in some senses I still do. My path of faith has wandered through both doubt and belief, often at the same time.

Doubt doesn't have to tear down belief, however; it can purify it. When it does, the beliefs on the other side become more certain. This is why I would like to affirm that it is possible to find God even while you are still asking the big questions.

The pivotal points in my own pilgrimage have occurred when I crossed thresholds of change—from inherited beliefs to intense questioning, from intense questioning to discovering what I truly believed and disbelieved. It is not an easy thing to let go of what is comfortable to make room for what is uncertain, but human life is a succession of such passages, from childhood through old age. I now find myself on such a threshold once again—and it is forcing me to both discover what I truly believe and examine whether I am truly living what I do believe.

As I approached my sixty-fifth birthday a few years ago, I experienced a strong urge to return to my religious roots in a new and fresh way—thoroughly reexamining what I believe and why. In part my motivation is a response to the many discussions I have had with secular friends and colleagues in which they inevitably ask, "So what do you really believe?" Indeed, the questions I have chosen to address in this book are some of those that keep coming up in these discussions. But this time I want to explore them with the same dedication I have brought to my vocation as a physician and medical journalist. The skills I have acquired in my scientific and journalistic experience should allow me to look more critically at my religious beliefs than I could have while in seminary forty years ago. But perhaps most importantly, I want to "cleanse" my beliefs to reveal their bedrock: to rediscover what I really do believe and then decide honestly what it means for how I live the rest of my life.

For nearly three decades I have been known to many television viewers as the medical editor of ABC News, on call for *Good Morning America* and other network news programs. As a physician I have committed my professional life to healing and wellness. A broadcasting career extended that commitment in ways I could never have foreseen. But my public work is only a small part of who I really am—or rather, who I want to be. This book is, in a sense, "the rest of my story." I hope that you might find in it some help and encouragement for your own process of spiritual exploration—whether or not you agree with the answers I affirm. Ultimately, you must find your own answers; other people's answers are never enough.

⸎

My story begins in Rockford, Illinois, in a fairly typical middle-class family—at least for Rockford in the 1930s. My family was very religious—in our case, members of a small Protestant denomination. The Evangelical Covenant Church originated in Sweden in the 1800s and was transplanted to this country, mostly to the Midwest, in the migrations of the latter part of that century. Our church in Rockford was a very big force in our family life, and my brother and I grew up knowing that God was a reality to be loved and trusted and that Jesus was the embodiment of God. My mother, particularly, was vocal about her faith—both verbally and musically—and radiated a deep trust in the goodness of God and the goodness of her fellow men and women.

So far, so good.

After graduating as valedictorian of my high school class, and much to the dismay of my high school guidance department, I chose to go to our church-sponsored college in Chicago, North Park Junior College. After the two years I transferred to Augustana College in Rock Island, Illinois. I majored in history and minored in philosophy, debated about what I wanted to do, and then decided to become a minister. Given my Christian upbringing and my writing and speaking abilities, it seemed like a perfectly natural choice.

Rather than proceeding immediately to our denominational seminary, also a part of North Park in Chicago, I went first for one semester to the University of Chicago Divinity School, sensing that it might be wise to gain a perspective different from the religious tradition I had been immersed in since childhood. I had no idea I would be challenged to the very core of my belief and being.

As I embarked on seminary studies, it struck me that if I were going to preach this stuff, I had really better believe it. But when I examined the claims of the Christian faith with that in mind, I found much that I couldn't easily accept or believe. In fact, under the challenge of some very bright and skeptical teachers at the University of Chicago, I began to doubt almost everything I had pretty much taken for granted: that the Bible is the Word of God, that Jesus was the Son of God and that God rules the universe (not to mention our world) and has a plan for it and for me.

In fact, I was so plagued by doubt that I became physically ill—not in a way that required medical treatment, but with symptoms of anxiety (sleeplessness and loss of appetite) caused by my "loss of faith." Fortuitously, I was able to make contact with Dr. Granger Westberg, a Lutheran minister and a pioneer in the hospital chaplain movement, who at that time was serving on the faculty of the divinity school and the staff of the medical center. I won't detail my path of spiritual recovery except to say that with time and the help of Dr. Westberg and several other persons of deep faith I encountered at the University, I slowly came to understand what I could believe—and to live with what I couldn't understand.

Ever since that time I have been comfortable with intellectual and spiritual doubt—and now I welcome it as a companion that stimulates me to think about what I really believe. I find that I need to continually explore the basis of my religious beliefs, that I cannot simply accept the teachings of theologians or the dogmas of the church. I have also been acutely aware that others who are very spiritual may have very different views than mine on the specifics of religious belief.

For example, during my study at the University of Chicago I first became both intellectually and emotionally aware of the real differences and profound similarities between Judaism and Christianity. I had been exposed to the stories of the "Old Testament" as part of the Christian Bible, but I had never really been exposed to the depth and beauty of Judaism until my time at the university; that exposure has continued throughout my life and has greatly influenced my spiritual perspective. The relatively short period of time I spent at the University of Chicago had a profound, lifelong impact on the way I look at religious claims of all kinds, including those of the tradition I was raised in.

After my semester at the university I returned to our denominational seminary and completed my divinity degree there. As part of the typical seminary training of that time, I spent time in a hospital setting. There I became increasingly drawn to the field of medicine and the way doctors could definitively and so often quickly be of help to people. The result was that two years after graduating from seminary I began medical school at age twenty-nine, fully expecting to become a family doctor and practice medicine in a small town the rest of my life.

But life held more surprises than I could possibly have imagined. Just weeks before graduating from medical school, I sat down one evening in the student lounge to watch the evening news on *The Huntley-Brinkley Report*. That particular day in the spring of 1969, the newscast reported on an American Medical Association (AMA) news conference announcing the organization's opposition to the proposed appointment of Dr. John Knowles as Assistant Secretary of Health Education and Welfare. He was then head of Massachusetts General Hospital in Boston (as you might guess, they disapproved of his "liberal" views on health care). The AMA trustee who conducted the press conference was so inept that when the program came back to Huntley and Brinkley, they were laughing out loud, and the newscast had to divert immediately to a commercial break. (I once asked the late David Brinkley, who had a long and distinguished tenure at ABC News, if he remembered that episode. There were so many incidents to laugh at in his career, he responded, that he couldn't remember that particular one.)

The very next day, by sheer coincidence, I received a form letter from the AMA inviting me to join the organization as a soon-to-be new doctor. On impulse I pulled a pen out of my pocket, wrote on the form letter something to the effect that if what I saw on the news the night before was any indication of their competence and policy, I wasn't interested. I mailed it back to them.

Much to my astonishment, several weeks later I received a personal letter from the executive director of the AMA, further outlining their opposition to Dr. Knowles. Much of what was said in the letter sounded off base to me. Again on impulse I sent the AMA letter to Dr. Knowles, whom I had never met, thinking he might be interested in what the AMA was saying about him.

It turned out that Dr. Knowles was very interested, and he wrote me back, asking permission to use the letter in a book he was thinking about writing. Several years later when I ended up working as a physician in Boston, I took the opportunity to meet Dr. Knowles personally, which led to an ongoing friendship. That happened to be just at the time that he was part of a group of Boston citizens who were taking over the operation of the ABC affiliate in Boston, WCVB-TV. At Dr. Knowles's request, I agreed to host a morning talk show on health and medicine for the public when the station went on the air in the spring of 1972. I continued to practice medicine and do part-time television work, joining *Good Morning America* when it started in 1975 and agreeing to join ABC News full time in 1984.

So the way I look at it, if I hadn't watched that particular newscast in 1969, I wouldn't be doing what I am today! I have thoroughly enjoyed my work in television, which has been stimulating and creative, and I have been blessed to work at a network that has given me enormous professional freedom. I would also like to believe that I have helped regular viewers of ABC News programs to live better and healthier lives. However, at this current season of my life — euphemistically described as the "onset of fall," perhaps more realistically described as "early winter" — I find myself swimming in waters with many conflicting currents: the continuing need to find answers to the big questions of life that are both intellectually and spiritually satisfying, a growing fascination with both the hard-nosed demands of scientific reasoning and the dramatic spiritual and ethical ideals found in the teachings of Jesus, and a growing anguish born of being materially privileged in a world of terrible suffering caused by poverty.

I am also aware that I am in a critical passage in my life for making decisions about how I will live the rest of it. Some of this uncertainty is undoubtedly age-related. But much of it arises from a growing conviction that I have not lived up to my own spiritual expectations, and therefore I should make some changes while I still have time. Thus this endeavor is far more than an intellectual or academic exercise for me. I feel as if this exploration is vital to my own spiritual health—and that it may trigger some unexpected changes in my life as a result. I am more eager than anyone to see how this all comes out!

I should confess right at the start that I have two strong biases, which may seem contradictory. On one hand, I really do want to believe that there is a God we can know and understand to our personal benefit. I am convinced, from both personal experience and the growing scientific data on the subject, that people of genuine religious faith and practice are likely to benefit from such faith in very practical ways, including better mental and physical health. But I also regard many of the claims made in the name of religion with an operative skepticism born and bred from my scientific training and experience, which has taught me to question any and all claims for "knowing the truth." These biases are not unlike what I bring to my attempts to evaluate claims for medical truth: I want to believe new claims of discoveries that might improve the human condition, but because of my long experience with premature or unfounded proclamations, I am inclined to be skeptical of them.

A second major bias consists of two basic assumptions I make about God: that we all have access to knowing God and that God is the author of all truth.

First, any entity worthy of that name must be available and at least partially knowable to all human beings, even though the "ways of knowing" might be quite different in various times and places. In short, a real God must be available to everyone, rather than merely a god of certain select or special people.

Second, I assume that God is the author of all truth—including new discoveries of all kinds. It would be highly unlikely that such a God would allow all other kinds of truth to unfold and expand in terms of our human understanding but insist that religious truth be completely understood only in one particular time or place. In other words, just as past medical knowledge was developed in the context of the culture and knowledge available at the time, so past religious and spiritual truth was developed in the context of that time. And just as medical knowledge has been updated and expanded by new knowledge and discovery, so I would expect that spiritual knowledge can also be enhanced in each new time and place. Depending on how these assumptions are interpreted, they can be quite controversial in some religious circles. But I am committed to seeing where they take me in the course of this writing.

Frankly, I am often surprised by some of my friends who basically have not thought about their religious beliefs since childhood and seemingly have no interest in doing so. They have essentially decided that what they learned in Sunday school or from official church teachings is good enough when it comes to religious beliefs. It reminds me of the attitude expressed on a bumper sticker to the effect of: "God said it. I believe it. That settles it." Most professionals would never dream of taking that attitude in presuming that what they learned decades ago in medical or graduate school is still adequate. But when it comes to religion, they seem to have concluded that the less they expose themselves to new ideas, the less they will rock their intellectual or spiritual boats, and the better off they will be.

Personally, I cannot imagine ignoring or avoiding modern scholarship of any kind, whether in medicine or religion. That doesn't

mean I agree with everything churned out by either scientific research or religious scholarship. But it does mean that I believe the
God of truth expects us to be open to new ideas and new research,
and honor the path of truth-seeking wherever it might lead. During
the past ten years I have spent most of my spare time reading on a
wide range of modern scholarship regarding the Christian religion,
the Bible and modern science. Indeed, my biggest problem in writing this book has been to stop reading and researching—which
could stretch out indefinitely—and just do it: write down what I believe and know at this point in my life. Those who believe they have
all the answers to religious questions, and those who think there are
no answers, won't be interested. But if you are like me, I would guess
that you want answers but remain skeptical about many of the answers you have heard. I hope you will find it helpful to dive into
some questions with me.

This book is organized in three sections that basically follow the
way my mind has always worked in coming to conclusions about my
spiritual beliefs. First, I begin by examining whether or not it makes
intellectual sense to believe that our world is designed by a creator
God rather than completely the result of chance. Therefore, the
next three chapters deal with the way we might discern God through
the study of nature, the phenomenon of life and the moral instincts
and relational drive of our human nature. If I can conclude that at
least it's not unreasonable to believe in a God of creation, then I am
more comfortable exploring the specific claims of my own religion,
the Christian faith.

Indeed, in today's world where so much evil is done in the cause
of religion and the name of God, it is mandatory to explain what our

"belief in God" means in more specific terms. Many American polls indicate that the majority of our citizens "believe in God." But as current world events so dramatically illustrate, the kind of God we believe in can differ astonishingly from one person to another.

The second section of this book is my way of explaining how I come to the specifics of my own belief in God. I will discuss some of the controversies surrounding the "historical Jesus" as well as his possible meaning for us today. I will also discuss some traditional Christian concepts and language that are often confusing to people with no background in the Christian faith. It doesn't help that Christian tradition, past and present, is rife with arguments and even violence among Christians who disagree with each other over doctrinal issues. How does a thoughtful person work through key questions about Christianity when Christians themselves fight over where to draw the lines around their claims for absolute answers?

After walking through the conclusions I have reached about a creator God and the significance of Jesus, the next major question concerns what such beliefs mean for the way I live my daily life. The third section explores practical implications arising from my own personal faith—with potentially life-changing challenges.

I firmly believe there are no more important questions than the ones I wrestle with in these three sections. Think about it: If there is a Creator who knows us and cares about how we live, then our lives should be profoundly affected. If there is a "history of the universe"—and if we have a personal "history" that continues after the termination of our earthly existence—then this experience we call "life" should take on a totally different meaning, far different than just surviving on earth for as long as and in the most luxurious fashion possible. In short, if our earthly life is only a small part of our journey, then shouldn't we be focusing on a much bigger picture than just our daily existence?

None of the sections in this book is even close to being exhaustive. It's not my goal to set forth a complete defense of religious belief, but simply to invite you to walk with me in a key season of my ongoing spiritual journey. I hope you find at least some of it helpful in coming to your own conclusions.

Finally, although this book is mostly about how to think through such questions, I believe it's the choices we make in our daily lives that tell our true story and reflect what we really believe. And if the truth be told, I have much less confidence in the human mind to figure out the mind of God than I did forty years ago and much more confidence in the mercy of God to tolerate our human explorations on these matters—maybe even to smile with satisfaction as would any good parent watching a child trying to figure it all out.

2

Is the Universe an Accident?

In one form or another, all questions about the meaning of existence can be reduced to one fundamental starting point: *Why is there something and not nothing?* Unless we simply take our existence for granted—which few people can afford to do, given the increasingly turbulent times in which we live—the world around us begs the question of how it came to be. Fortunately, there are now available to us, based on widely accepted scientific findings, some astounding observations about the nature and possible origins of the universe.

The Vastness and Complexity of the "External" Universe

If you have ever star-gazed on a clear evening far away from city lights, or peered into a microscope to view a reality your eyesight alone could never reveal to you, you know something of the sheer immensity and complexity of the universe.

A passage from a Thomas Hardy novel lyrically conveys a sense of this vast scale. In a midnight contemplation the lone viewer has a sense of riding "the roll of the world eastward," gliding along through the stars: "After such a nocturnal reconnoiter it is hard to get back to earth, and to believe that the consciousness of such majestic speeding is derived from a tiny human frame."[1]

But even when the human eye can capture images from beyond and within, we find it very difficult to put them into any kind of understandable perspective. We can do so only by constructing admittedly artificial comparisons and analogies that give us an intuitive glimpse of the world we find ourselves in.

The astonishing origin of the universe. The age of the universe is estimated to be anywhere from thirteen to fifteen billion years. That kind of time is incomprehensible. More staggering yet is the almost universally accepted scenario among cosmologists that in the blink of an eye, our current cosmos burst forth from a pinpoint of extremely dense and hot "quark-gluon plasma"—a primordial state of matter best described as a remarkably tiny dot of free-wheeling quark particles and the gluons binding them. This pinpoint of plasma expanded so rapidly the "event" has become widely known as the "big bang."

That term was first coined by the late British astronomer Fred Hoyle, who tackled some of the biggest questions in twentieth-century science. Later, in an international competition for a better name, the term survived over thirteen thousand proposed alternatives judged by a panel of my former ABC colleague Hugh Downs, the late astronomer Carl Sagan and the exceptional science writer Timothy Ferris.

Before the "bang," say the experts, there was no space—everything was contained in the pinpoint. Today, the process of space ex-

pansion continues as the galaxies in our cosmos are flung farther
away from each other. One obvious question is what preceded the
big bang, and what existed outside the "boundaries" of space as it
was exploding. When I put this to a friend who is a world-renowned
cosmologist, he started trying to explain to me the virtual vacuum-
concept before stopping with a smile and saying, "You just go back
to the beginning—and that's it."

The universe expanded for a billion or so years before galaxies
formed. It would be another 9 to 10 billion years before our solar system, including planet earth, came into existence. (For this purpose
I am ignoring the recent reported discovery of an anomalously ancient planet estimated to be a whopping 12.7 billion years old!) The
first evidence of simple unicellular life on earth is dated to about 3.5
billion years ago, but the major diversification of life into forms that
we would describe as animal life did not occur until less than a billion years ago. Dinosaurs first appeared on the scene about 250 million years ago, only to be wiped out, most likely from a large asteroid
invasion, about 190 million years later. More humanlike creatures
appeared "only" about 3.5 million years ago; the first truly human
species are dated to about one hundred thousand years ago.

You may be familiar with the celebrated time line transposing
this cosmic history into a single twenty-four-hour day, giving us a
more understandable frame of reference. If we are looking back at
the big bang starting upon the stroke of midnight, planet earth
would have formed at about the sixteen-hour point (four o'clock in
the afternoon). Human life would have emerged *less than one second* ago. On this scale, a lifetime of one hundred years takes up only
six ten-thousandths of a second.

Now for a more poetic version of the above cosmic history, by Stonehill College professor of physics Chet Raymo:

> The universe began 15 billion years ago with an explosion from an infinitely small mathematical singularity. The singularity was not "somewhere." The fabric of space-time came into existence with the explosion. There was no "before," at least none that we can presently know. Space swelled from the singularity like a balloon inflating from nothing.
>
> During the first trillion-trillion-trillionth of a second, matter and antimatter flickered in and out of existence. The fate of the universe hung precariously in the balance; it might grow, or it might collapse back into nothingness. Suddenly it ballooned to enormous size (after all, we are here), in what cosmologists call the inflationary epoch, bringing the first true particles of matter—the quarks—into existence. Within a millionth of a second the rapid swelling ceased, and the quarks began to be confined into protons, neutrons and electrons. The universe continued to expand and cool, but now at a more stately pace. Already the universe was vastly larger than what we are able to observe today. Within a few more minutes, protons and neutrons combined into the first atomic nuclei—hydrogen and helium—but still the universe was too hot for the nuclei to shag electrons and make atoms. Not until 300,000 years after the beginning did the first atoms appear.
>
> Irregularities in the gassy universe of hydrogen and helium were accentuated by gravity. Within a billion years after the beginning, the first stars and galaxies were born. There were not yet any Earthlike planets orbiting the stars of the earliest galaxies, because there were not yet significant quantities of the heavy elements (these would be cooked up later in stars). Nor had the Sun yet been born. But within a few billion years, the universe had begun to look familiar on the largest scale.[2]

I cannot resist pointing out what others have also observed: if this specific scenario had been proposed in any of the world's holy books, it would have been dismissed as fanciful myth.

But because this description of the origin of life has come from the mouths of scientists, it is widely accepted as "gospel truth." Go figure.

The incredible scope of "outer" space. How can I possibly convey the size of our cosmos as presently understood by cosmologists? First, try to grasp the meaning of the speed of light by envisioning its travel across the length of the United States. Knowing that light in a vacuum travels at the speed of 186,000 miles per second, you can divide that number by 3,000 (distance in miles across the country) to conclude that in just *one second,* light can travel back and forth across the United States *sixty-two times!*

With that sense of distance per second, you can describe the moon as being 1.3 light seconds (240,000 miles) away from earth, and the sun as being 8.3 light minutes (93 million miles) away from earth. Now try to imagine the distance light can travel in one hour, then one day and finally in one year—which happens to be six trillion miles! Now with that already unimaginable distance in mind, consider the kinds of distances in terms of light years (remember: six trillion miles in just *one* year) that cosmologists use to describe the hierarchical structure of the universe:

- A single galaxy can be many thousands of light years across in diameter. For example, our galaxy, the Milky Way, is a system of about 400 billion stars that is some *ninety to one hundred thousand* light years in diameter.

- A cluster, which can contain hundreds or thousands of galaxies, can be *millions* of light years in diameter.

- A supercluster can be up to a few *hundred million* light years across.

- Walls or sheets (sometimes called supercluster complexes) can stretch for a *billion* light years.[3]

Today, when we consider the "heavens above," we are facing an impossible task compared to our ancient ancestors, for whom the stars were close companions in a familiar night sky.

But impossible as it is to grasp the scope of the cosmos, it may be even more difficult to understand the structure and function of the universe within.

THE VASTNESS AND COMPLEXITY
OF THE INTERNAL UNIVERSE

Most of us grew up understanding the atom to be a stable and simple structure—a little ball in the middle called the *nucleus* (composed of protons and neutrons), plus specks called *electrons* spinning about the nucleus in various orbits. No longer! Today, the atomic and subatomic worlds, what I am informally calling the "internal universe," are best understood as clouds of uncertainty every bit as mind-boggling as the spaces of the cosmos.

Let's begin with the structure of the simplest of atoms, hydrogen—first in the periodic table because it consists of a nucleus of one proton with one orbiting electron. However, even though both of these components are unimaginably small, there is an enormous distance between the nucleus and its electron.

Try to grasp this: The radius of a hydrogen nucleus is about 10^{-15} meters. That's a 1 with fourteen zeros between it and the decimal point, and it would look like this:

.0000000000000001

In other words, it's very, very small!

However, that radius is about 1/50,000 of the distance between the nucleus and the electron. In other words, even as tiny as the hydrogen atom is (so tiny we cannot comprehend it) it is *mostly space*. (And by implication, any "solid" object, like a piece of wood, is really mostly space even though it's hard for us to believe it as we hold, it or try to pound a nail into it.)

This concept of atoms as mostly space is ultimately impossible to grasp. Timothy Ferris points out that if it were not for the negatively charged fields of two "solid" objects (like billiard balls) that cause them to repel each other, they could quite literally pass through each other "unscathed."[4] And the modern picture of atoms would have to be painted in very different strokes than that of the model we have been describing. As Bill Bryson puts it in his wonder-filled book *A Short History of Nearly Everything*, "The electron doesn't fly around the nucleus like a planet around its sun, but instead takes on the more amorphous aspect of a cloud. . . . The cloud itself is essentially just a zone of statistical probability. . . . This atom, if you could see it, would look more like a very fuzzy tennis ball than a hard-edged metallic sphere."[5] And these structural clouds lead us into a brief exploration of some of the cloudy concepts of modern physics.

The incredible complexity of "inner" space. I am about to offer you an even bigger headache: a snippet of the truly incomprehensible ideas generated by the relatively new concepts of quantum physics. Let me warn you up front that you will not be able to grasp emotionally much of what I am about to report, and neither can I. So let's all take comfort from one of the founders of quantum thought, the remarkable Danish physicist Niels Bohr, who reportedly said, "If anybody says that he can think about quantum problems without getting giddy, that shows only that he has not understood the first thing about them."[6]

The word *quantum* derives from the Latin word for "packet" or "packages" and refers to subatomic units of energy called "quanta" (singular "quantum"). But quantum physics doesn't speak of definite locations, speeds and paths for these packets, like classical physics does for the large, everyday objects in our universe. Instead, quantum physics speaks of "chances" and "probabilities" and further insists that the very act of observing or measuring quantum energy packets will change them, meaning we can never know precisely what or where something at the subatomic level really is or where it is going.

The famous Heisenberg Uncertainty Principle says that it is impossible to measure both the position and movement of a quantum packet at the same time: the more accurate the measurement of *position*, the less accurate the measurement of *movement*—and vice versa. (To make matters even more complicated, sometimes these "events" will be wavelike, sometimes they will be particlelike, depending on how you observe them.) One conclusion from this uncertainty is that scientists can never predict exactly what the outcome of a given quantum event will be; they can speak only of probabilities. (It is much like the work of actuaries in the insurance industry; they can never predict when a given person will die, but they can very accurately predict the overall results for a large group of people.)

However, if you think uncertainty is unsettling, there is another quantum concept that really shakes the brain. Very reputable quantum physicists claim they have proven that once any two quantum particles have interacted, they can subsequently influence each other *no matter how widely they are separated.* In other words, if two electrons interact in a lab and one stays in the lab and the other ends up in outer space somewhere, anything that affects the one in the lab will immediately affect the other in outer space! That seems to require instant communication beyond the speed of light—even though, according to the theory of relativity, that is impossible. If you find this impossible to understand or believe, don't feel bad; Einstein couldn't either and said it showed there was something wrong with quantum theory. However, recent experiments have confirmed that this is the way the subatomic quantum world functions.[7]

One more mind bender: According to the Hubble European Space Agency, cosmologists estimate that what we can "see" in our universe accounts for only about 15 to 20 percent of the "matter" that is actually out there. Where or what is the other 80 to 85 percent? One recent guess is stuff called WIMPS—Weakly Interacting Massive Particles. Nonetheless, despite their massive size, they can supposedly pass through visible objects—including us. In other words, according to this theory much of the dark stuff we can't see because it doesn't emit light is composed of WIMPS, which can pass right through the solid objects we *can* see.

I have only skipped across the surface of some of the amazing things we are learning about the universe. They are way outside the boundaries of ordinary thought and experience, dazzling even the most brilliant minds into head-shaking guesswork. But all this discovery simply intensifies the question of how all this mind-bending reality came into existence.

DID IT HAPPEN BY CHANCE OR DESIGN?

When we encounter an object of everyday life, whether a painting or an airplane, we automatically assume that it was made or "created" by a human mind—or a committee of human minds. We know that such objects don't just appear by chance from an unplanned gathering of bits and pieces of substance that happen to join and organize into a recognized and functioning object. Our whole life experience has conditioned us to assume that things exist because somebody created them.

But even if our immediate instinct as a child is to feel or believe that some kind of mind was ultimately responsible for this cosmos of ours, we can soon be argued into thinking that maybe the whole thing did indeed happen by accident, so to speak. Why is it that we would never accept that argument for the simplest of objects, yet we are so quick to assent to the proposition that the most remarkable "object" of all is a product of chance?

While growing up I knew that once I started asking the big questions, such as "Who made God?" and "What existed before the beginning?" I was in trouble—because once you start them up, there's no way to shut them down. No matter how hard I tried—and I spent lots of time daydreaming in childhood trying—I couldn't come up with understandable answers. I eventually learned to put the impossible questions aside to focus on those I thought I possibly could answer. Of all of them, there is one question that in varying forms has always been central for me: Is this world as we know it more likely a result of *design* (a plan) or *chance* (an accident)? In fact, almost every day of my adult life I have been stimulated to ask this question. You will probably not be surprised by my ultimate answer: I find it more plausible to believe that our world is the result of design than to believe it happened by accident.

But that does not mean such belief comes easily, and I will share some of my struggles on this particular question with you. (I would also refer you to the books listed in "Suggested Reading"; they will give you far more information and reasoning than I will in this much shorter and personal version of wrestling with this question.)

The question of chance. I should first pose the obvious question: Could the universe as we know it have happened by chance? And if we are willing to put any religious belief aside, the answer is yes. Since we do not yet know in any absolutely certain way how or why this universe came to be, if we are honest we have to admit the theoretical possibility that everything we know about our universe could have happened by chance. So the real question I wrestle with is this: *What are the chances it has all happened by chance?* Or to be more elegant, *What is the probability that the universe as we now know it happened by chance rather than by design?*

In facing this question it might be helpful to consider a widely quoted parable, a scenario in which you are about to be executed. You are tied to a stake and the order is given for a contingent of highly trained marksmen to fire. The shots ring out but you find you have survived.

What do you conclude? Were you incredibly lucky that all of these highly trained individuals just happened to miss at the same time? Or did the marksmen or their superiors plan for this remarkable coincidence to have happened?

First, let's face directly one of the usual arguments for chance, namely, that with enough time, anything—including this universe—could result from accidental interactions between the forces and substances evolving from the big bang. One persistent analogy supporting this hypothesis is the famous "monkey argument," supposedly introduced by the British scientist A. S. Eddington, suggesting that an army of monkeys pounding on typewriters might eventually write all the books in the British Museum if given enough time. (T. H. Huxley's version of this argument had monkeys eventually typing the works of Shakespeare.)

However, as Patrick Glynn argues in his very readable book *God: The Evidence*,[8] this analogy quickly falls apart when you think of it more logically. Every time a monkey starts typing, he is at ground zero, so even if a word or two results from his random pecking, the possibility that a complete book—let alone an entire universe—could result is statistically ludicrous. Or to use Glynn's observation, it would have to be regarded as a "miracle."[9] Even if, on a given day, a monkey picking at the keys happened to type a few words, that would not mean the monkey was on a roll and that simply given enough time it would come up with a Shakespearean play. Actually, the reality is that the very next moment the monkey would be starting over and would be lucky just to come up with a few words again.

For me, the most dramatic analogy of the improbability of chance alone accounting for life as we know it comes from the same Fred Hoyle who coined the term "big bang": "The chance that higher life forms might have emerged in this way is comparable with the chance that 'a tornado sweeping through a junk-yard might assemble a Boeing 747 from the material therein.' "[10] Considering the range of coincidences necessary for human life—from crucial cosmic distances to subatomic clouds colliding appropriately—even this junkyard analogy seems woefully inadequate (see chap. three).

But what about Darwin's concept of natural selection as an explanation of the development of life, including the human species? Isn't that well-documented phenomenon a perfect argument for the possibility of chance resulting in outcomes of incredible sophistication?

That's a legitimate question. However, it skips over a crucial fact: *Darwin had nothing to say about the most unfathomable phenomenon of all*—namely, the development of living cells from the nonliving chemicals resulting from the big bang and its byproducts. How could he? He knew nothing about these matters. However, Darwin intuitively anticipated the possibility that this kind of biochemical complexity could dramatically challenge the idea of natural selection as a complete explanation for the origins of the living world. In his *Origin of Species* he wrote, "If it could be demonstrated that any complex organ existed which could not possibly have been formed by numerous, successive, slight modifications, my theory would absolutely break down."[11] I personally think that Darwin was being overly dramatic in suggesting that such discoveries would cause his theory to "absolutely break down." But I do think the transformation of dead chemicals from the scattered cosmic residue of the big bang into living cells cannot, at least yet, be easily explained by the concept of natural selection, which works so well in the world of already living organisms.

However, I accept that the human race has been shaped by millions of years of life evolving from very simple forms of life into the kind of complex organism we know today. I also believe that during this evolution, the process of natural selection has played a definitive role. But I do not think we can equate the process of natural selection—the generational transmission of genetic mutations that favor survival—with mere chance. Rather, I believe that *natural selection has worked only because the underlying design of the universe has made it possible.* In other words, I don't see any discoveries of modern science, including natural selection, as a threat to the basic idea that there is some kind of intelligence at work in the unfolding of this incredible universe we inhabit.

In the next chapter we will look at "cosmic coincidences," indicating that the universe is particularly configured to support life on our planet. Without such conditions it would have been impossible for life as we know it to be shaped by the process we label natural selection. Put bluntly, there would have been nothing from which to select, because the genetic and chemical shelves would have been bare.

Another reason why it seems impossible to account for the complexity of life completely through chance is the complex machinery of cellular genetics, which I will also explore in the next chapter. This intricate process at the microlevel is what allows mutations to take place—and, more importantly, preserves them to be passed on to future generations. Without these genetic mechanisms, natural selection could not occur—and evolution as it is conventionally understood would be dead in its tracks.

I love the way John Polkinghorne describes the interplay of chance and what he calls "necessity" in the phenomenon of natural selection:

> Genetic mutations are happenstance; they just occur from time to time. Thus, there arise new forms of life that are sifted and preserved by natural selection in an orderly environment. *If genetic information were unchangingly transmitted from generation to generation, nothing new*

*would ever happen, and, if it were not reasonably reliable in its trans-
mission, nothing would ever be perpetuated.* A fertile world must be
neither too rigid, nor too loose. It needs both chance and necessity.[12]
(italics mine)

I agree with his highlighting of the interaction of chance and
necessity; it is a theme I will return to later in this book when I discuss the question of providence. However, I would gently quarrel
with his use of the words *just occur* as an adequate explanation of the
phenomenon of so-called genetic mutations. I believe that this phenomenon fits into the category of designed mechanisms, which allow chance or spontaneity to play a role in ongoing evolution.

In summary, I believe that the vastness and complexity of our inner and outer universes argue *against* chance as a total explanation
for the universe as we know it today. Quite the contrary, the more we
learn, the less likely it seems that it could all have "just happened."
And for me the most convincing argument that the universe has
been "designed" is the extraordinary way it is calibrated to allow for
the genesis and continuation of life itself.

3

How Did We Get Here?

✤

It's one thing to gaze at the big picture of the universe and presume that it happened by chance—after all, thought buckles at the attempt to understand its vastness and complexity. If we can't even fathom what's there, how could we fathom the fantastic origins responsible for its existence? Quite frankly, I'm often tempted to give up trying and dismiss it with a mental shrug—*the whole thing is just beyond understanding; somehow, it happened.*

However, when we are looking specifically at the incredible circumstances that have allowed human life to come into existence, a new question confronts us: How did *we* get here? Are we dazzling yet inexplicable specks of dust in a random universe, or are we the result of careful design, and are we *supposed* to be here?

Cosmic Coincidences?

To make connections between the patterns of the universe and the existence of life, I will begin first with some of the *coincidences of the cosmos.* Another term for these observations is *contingencies,* meaning that the existence of life is contingent on such conditions being in place.

One example is the frequent self-destructive explosion of stars. These fiery furnaces manufacture the elements essential for life (carbon, nitrogen, oxygen, iron, etc.) and scatter them throughout the cosmos as stardust, which eventually accumulates in planets such as earth. The explosions also generate shock waves that may be critical to the condensation of cosmic gas and dust into planetary systems such as our own solar system. If these explosions occur too close to a planet, however, they can destroy it. And if the planets formed were too close to each other, they could destabilize orbits. The distance between planets in our solar system is about 30 million miles, just the right distance for stable orbits.[1]

The fundamental forces of nature provide another instance of cosmic contingencies. For example, the initial explosive force of the big bang appears to have been "just right" to result in the formation of the universe. The most unfathomably microscopic shift one way or another—for example, a change in strength of the force by as little as one part in 10^{59} (a "1" followed by 59 zeros), and the universe would have either collapsed back on itself or expanded too rapidly for stars to form. And according to one expert, an accuracy of this magnitude can be compared to firing a bullet at a one-inch target on the other side of the observable universe, twenty billion light years away, and hitting the target![2]

Physicists classify the four fundamental forces of nature as gravitational, electromagnetic, strong nuclear and weak nuclear. Each one influences specific particles—for example, the strong nuclear force binds together protons and neutrons in the nucleus of an atom. Now consider the following coincidences in these forces of nature, which permit life to exist:

- If gravity were just 10^{33} times weaker than electromagnetism instead of 10^{39} times weaker, stars would burn a *million times faster*, making it impossible for them to produce the heavy elements necessary for life.

- If the nuclear weak force were just slightly weaker in relation to gravity, most of the hydrogen in the universe would have been turned into helium, with profound consequences—such as no water.

- If the so-called nuclear strong force were just 2 percent stronger, it would have prevented the formation of protons—meaning a universe with no atoms. If it had been 5 percent weaker, we would have a universe with no stars and therefore no elements necessary for carbon-based life.[3]

It is precisely these "fundamental constants" imbedded in the forces of nature that have driven several agnostic (religiously speaking) physicists to consider the possibility of a "designer" for our universe. Among them is the noted physicist and writer Paul Davies, who states:

> It is hard to resist the impression that the present structure of the universe, apparently so sensitive to minor alterations in the numbers, has been rather carefully thought out. . . . Perhaps future developments in science will lead to more direct evidence for other universes, but until then, the seemingly miraculous concurrence of numerical values that nature has assigned to her fundamental constants must remain the most compelling evidence of an element of cosmic design.[4]

CAN YOU MAKE A HUMAN BY ACCIDENT?

However, for me the more understandable and fascinating contingencies are to be found in the remarkable story of human life—a "universe" with which I am more familiar and comfortable, given my own training as a physician. For this section I am relying heavily on a book titled *Nature's Destiny* by Michael J. Denton, a senior research fellow in human molecular genetics at the University of Otago in New Zealand.[5] The book draws on Dr. Denton's training as both a physician and a cellular biologist by synthesizing a remarkable variety of information from the biological sciences to support his thesis: *both the macroworld of the cosmos and the microworld of biochemistry are fine-tuned to lead to the fascinating biological phenomenon we call homo sapiens.* As he points out, this thesis is much more supportable today than in the past, when we knew so little about this universe that it seemed to be a vast screen on which the human race appeared as an accidental speck.

Today the exploding knowledge about the universe seems to me increasingly supportive of the notion that human life is an inevitable outcome and that the universe is full of amazing coincidences that make such life possible. To give you a taste of these remarkable phenomena, I will summarize some of the more compelling (at least to me) data, reduced in complexity, from Denton's marvelous book.

At this point I want to issue a word of caution: for those of you who don't enjoy reading about scientific matters, especially regarding human biology, feel free to skip the following two sections: "An environment that makes human life possible" and "A secret code that makes human life replicable." This material may be too technical for some, and you can easily follow my reasoning without reading these sections. Alternatively, you might quickly skim this material to get a brief idea of the topics covered. (If you want to jump ahead, start at page 53, "Did the Universe Have Us in 'Mind'?")

An environment that makes human life possible. I invite you to stop and think right now about some of the most basic components of your environment that are essential to your existence. I am going to choose just four whose silent actions and interactions make it possible for you to take your next breath and continue to enjoy the privilege of being alive while you read these words.

WATER. We all take water for granted—until we are thirsty. Then for a fleeting moment until our thirst is satisfied, we viscerally grasp the significance of water. But even then, we really have no idea just how important water is to our moment-by-moment existence—or how uniquely suited it is for life.

First, consider water's thermal (temperature-related) properties. We know that if water did not have the unique property of contracting as it gets colder until *just before* freezing, when it dramatically reverses course and expands, then the waters of the world would freeze solid from the bottom up. That, of course, would be a disaster for all aquatic life—and therefore for us!

Next, consider water's unique role as "universal solvent." Better than any other known liquid, it permits almost all known reactions while itself being just reactive enough to avoid becoming involved in destructive fashion—as is the case with liquids like acids and alkalis.

And then there is the viscosity or "stickiness" of water. If water were any less sticky, it would be less stable and could therefore disrupt delicate cellular activities. But if water were more viscous, it would prevent the movement of large molecules necessary for cell division. Water's viscosity is precisely ideal for the flow of blood components from capillaries to nearby cells; without the appropriate flow of oxygen and sugar to cells, life would quickly cease.

LIGHT. Step outside in ideal weather, and what is one of your first sensations? It is bound to be the bright warmth of sunlight on your face. Without enough of this, you will be physically and emotionally deprived. Too much of this, and you will sustain severe, perhaps even life-threatening, damage.

Our universe is constantly bathed in electromagnetic radiation—waves of energy that vary in the wavelength (the distance between two wave crests) from radio waves, which are several kilometers apart, to gamma rays, which are less than a trillionth of a centimeter apart. However, the majority of the electromagnetic radiation produced by the sun is found in a very small wavelength range from the near ultraviolet through the visible light range (what our eye can process) to the near infrared. And that is precisely the range needed to provide the energy for the great majority of chemical reactions that occur in living creatures. And here is the real kicker: the electromagnetic radiation in other wavelengths is very dangerous to human life.

But there is more. Our atmosphere, composed largely of oxygen, nitrogen and carbon dioxide gases plus water vapor, allows this friendly radiation to reach us—and largely blocks the dangerous stuff like gamma and X radiation. Further, the spectrum of radiation reaching earth is vitally important for photosynthesis—that plant process we learned about in high school biology—which generates the carbon fuels necessary for the oxidation that provides energy for the human body. This radiation is also critically important for the high-quality human vision that has fueled the intellectual development of homo sapiens.

CARBON. For good reason, human life is often described as carbon based: without the carbon atom, human life as we know it would be impossible. Carbon is the building block for almost all of life's essential processes. But why is carbon so uniquely suited for life? Here are just a few of the reasons.

Chemically, the carbon atom is ideally suited to form stable bonds with many of the other readily available elements in our universe. With hydrogen it forms hydrocarbons—such compounds as natural gas, petroleum, gasoline, greases and waxes. With hydrogen and oxygen it forms sugars, cellulose, fatty acids and beeswax. With hydrogen, oxygen and nitrogen it forms the building blocks of proteins (the amino acids). And the atoms which were among the first to be made by stars—and which are now among the most abundant in the cosmos—are carbon, oxygen, hydrogen and nitrogen!

Carbon offers a perfect balance between stability (allowing so many compounds to be formed and maintained) and flexibility (allowing many reactions and changes to occur). However, this balance occurs only within a rather narrow temperature range—which just happens to be that temperature range of our earthly environment, a very narrow fraction in the temperature range in our universe. By the way, this earthly temperature range also happens to be the one in which water remains in liquid form, versus ice or steam.

OXYGEN. The process of oxidation provides an astounding amount of energy in precisely controlled fashion. Given the dangerously reactive combustibility of oxygen—as evidenced in an out-of-control fire—it is surprising that oxidation in the human body is so safe and effective. As you might expect, there are reasons for this.

First, if the *amount* of oxygen in the air we breathe were more than 21 percent, not only would there be greatly increased dangers from environmental fires (according to Denton, the probability of a forest fire being ignited by lightning increases by as much as 70 percent for every 1 percent increase in atmospheric oxygen), but there also would be a greatly increased risk of oxidation damage to body tissues. The 21 percent threshold turns out to be the point at which benefit and risk are nicely balanced.

Second, oxidation in the body is tempered because the *high combustibility* of oxygen is offset by the *low combustibility* of carbon. You can see this phenomenon by building a fire in a fireplace. The initial difficulty of getting the wood to catch fire is due to wood's composition of largely carbon compounds. In addition, at normal body temperatures, oxygen exists in a molecular form combining two oxygen atoms, which makes it less volatile.

Finally, the *solubility* of oxygen (that is, its ability to dissolve in water) and the *diffusion* of oxygen (its ability to move in water) are just right for the necessary transport in blood so oxygen can generate energy through fueling body metabolism.

This brief summary of the unique qualities of water, light, carbon and oxygen gives us a glimpse of how remarkably the basic elements of our environment act and interact to make our existence possible. Now let's invert our focus to the microscopic world of the human cell. Here we'll look at the "inside" story of how the universe produces building blocks for human life.

A *secret code that makes human life replicable*. By now most everyone knows the dramatic story of the discovery of the structure of DNA—the double-stranded helix carrying the entire genetic code of an organism in every cell. It is DNA that also allows that cell to divide while making an exact full copy of the code for each of the two resulting new cells. Indeed, my own view is that this constant and precise replication of the genetic code in cells and organisms is a greater miracle than the actual origin of life. It is one thing to have arrived at the incredibly complicated organism known as a human being. It is quite another to replicate the exquisite complexity of that organism anew in each generation. The heroes of our story are DNA and, what may be the most amazing of all the chemical structures in our universe, proteins.

Consider the structure and function of DNA. Every cell in our body—from the cells in a strand of hair to those in the muscles of the heart to the neurons of the brain—contains a string of genetic material about one meter long (about the length of a human arm) coiled into a tiny ball five thousandths of a millimeter in diameter! *Every time* a cell divides, this coiled strand unzips down the middle into two strands; then each forms a partner strand. The result is two new cells, each containing the entire human genetic code which— thanks to the human genome project—we now know consists of over three billion "letters," containing the blueprint for an entire new human being!

Now consider just one example of what routinely comes out of that tiny genetic ball in each new human: the most amazing organ of all, the human brain. We know it is the most complicated human organ anatomically: billions of individual cells called neurons connected by trillions of chemical transmitting junctures called synapses. But even though we have begun to understand the brain's structure in minimal ways, we still have no idea how it functions to produce such phenomena as thinking and feeling. Don't confuse the fact that we have a vague idea of *where* these activities occur with an understanding of *how* they occur.

Fortunately, DNA structure has several properties ideally suited to its task of "producing" such structures as the brain — including

- Appropriate *chemical stability*, allowing it both to remain stable during the everyday life of the cell and to be pulled apart during cell division. If the bonds between the two strands were stronger, they would be frozen in what Denton describes as "an immobile, lifeless embrace."[6] If they were weaker, the molecule would disintegrate, as would the function and structure of the cell.

- *Compacting ability*, allowing a very long strand to coil into a very tiny ball. This means that *all* of the information needed to run a complex human organism weighs less than a *few trillionths* of a gram. Denton points out that if we were to collect *all* of the information needed to specify the design of *all the organisms that have ever existed on the planet*, it could easily fit into the size of a grain of salt![7] That requires belief simply to imagine, doesn't it?

However, the most important property of DNA leads us to the protein story: DNA geometry is perfect for allowing it to communicate with proteins, the amazing chemicals that form the structures of the cell as well as direct its activities. Here is how Denton describes the role of proteins:

Building atom by atom, they assembled over eons of time every living structure that ever existed on earth. They built the first cell; they built the human brain; they erected the dinosaurs and all past life on earth. All the vital chemical functions of every cell on earth are all dependent on the activities of those tiny nanomachines. The living kingdom, in a very real sense, has its being and origin in the infinitely rich, ever-changing patterns woven from the interactions of these tiny fragile collections of dancing atoms, a billion times smaller than the tiniest visible speck of dust.[8]

The enormous flexibility and variability of proteins allows them to perform amazing duties in the cell, ranging from building actual structures, such as the cornea of the eye or a muscle tendon, to serving as the creative participants in chemical processes known as catalysts. They also act as the chemical messengers in a cell, being formed in one location and then traveling to another to cause a reaction or function. And they do all of this without any external direction from other cell chemicals!

In short, DNA and proteins seem to be perfectly suited to the interacting tasks of information transmittal and cell communication. They pass the torch of genetic instruction from cell to cell and then translate that information into cell structure and function.

DID THE UNIVERSE HAVE US IN "MIND"?

One of the casualties of the Copernican Revolution (which proved that our solar system revolved around the sun, not the earth) was the previously accepted view of Greek cosmology that the earth was the center of the universe. Actually, based on the tools of observation available, it was a reasonable conclusion at the time. As the discoveries of the next four centuries accumulated, however, this conclusion gave way to the common observation that we live on a tiny planet orbiting an insignificant star in a minor galaxy, all of it floating in an infinite void.

However, the discoveries of the twentieth century produced a slow but steady trend toward the recognition of the special place of earth in the universe and the special nature of humanity among life on earth.

As it turns out, it is no longer scientifically significant that the earth is not the astronomical center of the known universe, because it is now clear that there is no spatial center in our cosmos. Our apparently insignificant place in the universe turns out to be quite ideal for the development of our species. In fact, contemporary science is telling us that it takes a universe as large and as long in the making as ours to allow for the development of the precise conditions necessary for life such as ours.

Indeed, so impressive is the information discovered in the past century that some scientists have even ventured to talk about these coincidences as a matter of "principle"—a recurring theme built into the very fabric of our cosmos. In 1973 a group of eminent scientists gathered in Poland to observe the 500th birthday of Copernicus. Brandon Carter, a colleague of Stephen Hawking, presented a daring paper on the growing evidence that the laws of physics and biology seemed "designed" to result in human life as we know it—the so-called *anthropic principle.*[9] Since that time the invocation of the anthropic principle has become common in discussions about "chance" versus "design." And even though it has an obvious anthropocentric flavor (seeing the world through our own point of view), it has gained considerable favor as more and more coincidences are discovered.

I want to mention one obvious critique of this reasoning—namely, that we should not be surprised by the appearance of an anthropic design in our universe *because by definition it is the only kind of universe that could be* IF *we exist.* In other words, we exist only because we are in a kind of universe that "allows" and "encourages" our existence. This may seem like classic circular reasoning, but I think it deserves recognition as a valid statement. However, the fact that this is a logical or valid statement says nothing about whether it argues *for* or *against* design. In fact, this statement says nothing about origins. It simply states the obvious in a descriptive (end result) rather than interpretive (process) sense.

For me the question then becomes, *To what degree or in what manner does the universe seem to mesh with the human experience?* If so-called anthropic coincidences simply allowed a basic protoplasmic existence, I couldn't get too excited—and, of course, our minds wouldn't have evolved to the point of even appreciating this argument. But maybe our minds are indeed a reflection of the "mind of God" in the sense of our ability even to begin fathoming the mysteries of the universe.

The incomparable Einstein observed that for him the only *incomprehensible* part of the universe was that it was *comprehensible.* In a different way I think he was asking the ultimate question, the one I have been trying to wrestle with in this section: *Does the fact that humans can even presume to understand the cosmos, as we now do, say anything about its origin and our place in it?* It would be one thing to have enough knowledge to survive while shivering before a fire in a cave. It is quite another phenomenon to understand, as Einstein first did, that mass and energy can actually bend or curve space and time.

The reason we can so reason—or at least, the reason some people can!—is that we humans can understand and appreciate the beauty and language of mathematics, which seems to be the language of the universe. Again I turn to John Polkinghorne to articulate a complex observation:

> When we use mathematics in this way—as the key to unlocking the secrets of the universe—something very strange is happening. . . . So, what ties together the reason within (the mathematics in our heads), and the

reason without (the structure of the physical world)? Remember. It's a
very deep connection, going far beyond anything we need for everyday
survival. . . . What I've been saying is that the universe, in its rational
beauty and transparency, looks like a world shot through with signs of
mind, and, maybe, it's the "capital M" Mind of God we are seeing. In
other words, the reason within and the reason without fit together because they have a common origin in the reason of the Creator, who is the
ground of all that is.[10]

God to Earth?

But all this complexity raises an obvious question: If there were a
God who has designed the universe to result in human beings, why
would this God choose to remain so hidden? Why would God be so
subtle as to communicate in an obtuse fashion—such as the language of mathematics—instead of disclosing divinity in a more obvious and universal fashion?

It is reported that the famous English mathematician and atheist
Bertrand Russell (author of *Why I Am Not a Christian*) was asked on
his deathbed what he would say if he discovered after death that in
fact there was a God. He supposedly replied, "I think I should say to
him: Sir, it appears that my atheistic hypothesis was erroneous.
Would you mind answering me one wee little question? Why didn't
you give us more evidence?"[11] It is worth pausing at this point to consider that question. If there is a God who designed this universe, why
didn't that God make it all crystal clear—so obvious that humankind
would not have to struggle so hard and so long to figure it out? In
other words, at some point, why didn't (doesn't) God do something
to make the answers to all the questions about the origin and meaning of life more obvious?

Consider Woody Allen's amusing response to this dilemma: "If only God would give me some clear sign! Like making a large deposit in my name at a Swiss bank."[12] Okay, let's assume God did just that. Do you think it would persuade Mr. Allen, or anyone else, of God's existence? Personally, I doubt it. I think most people would instead believe some other explanation—such as an error by the bank.

But what about a more serious suggestion from Norwood Russell Hanson, the late philosopher of science at Yale, who described what it would take to make him believe in God?

> The conditions are these: Suppose, next Tuesday morning, just after breakfast, all of us in this one world are knocked to our knees by a percussive and ear-shattering thunderclap. . . . The sky is ablaze with an eerie silvery light, and just then, as all of the people of this world look up, the heavens open and the clouds pull apart, revealing an unbelievably radiant and immense Zeus-like figure towering over us like a hundred Everests. He frowns darkly as lightning plays over the features of his Michelangeloid face, and then he points down at me, and explains for every man, woman, and child to hear: "I've had quite enough of your too-clever logic chopping and word-watching in matters of theology. Be assured, Norwood Russell Hanson, that I do most certainly exist."[13]

Okay, that would do it for me too, as it probably would for any human awake (and sober) at the time. But is that really what we want—being forced to believe by being brought to our knees in intellectual and spiritual servitude? What kind of God would act like that, bullying us into acceptance? Would that kind of "belief" be meaningful, if we hadn't chosen it?

Danish philosopher Søren Kierkegaard told a story about the dilemma of a king who falls in love with a peasant girl. How can he convey his love without destroying the possibility of a freely chosen relationship on her part? Obviously, he can't simply order her to love him. And if he showers her with gifts, he can never know if she loves him for his own sake. The king finally decides that the best way is to put aside his rank and woo her in disguise.

Indeed, thinking about how God could become known to us without destroying our essence as autonomous creatures points out how tricky this question of knowing God really is.

The remarkable French scientist and amateur theologian Blaise Pascal addresses this very question in his wonderful collection of musings, *The Pensées*. In one typically pithy section he writes, "God wishes to move the will rather than the mind. Perfect clarity would help the mind and harm the will."[14] In other words, God could make it all obvious, but at a terrible price—the loss of what makes us human, the ability to choose freely rather than submit passively, the possibility of being wise rather than dumbstruck.

However, there is often a price exacted for this freedom of the mind: an intellectual anxiety that can be deeply disturbing to a sensitive and searching human being. Indeed, the message of the "hidden God" in nature can be so annoyingly ambiguous as to drive a thinking person to a kind of spiritual madness, as it apparently did for Pascal:

> This is what I see and what troubles me. I look around in every direction and all I see is darkness. Nature has nothing to offer me that does not give rise to doubt and anxiety. If I saw no sign there of a Divinity I should decide on a negative solution; if I saw signs of a Creator everywhere I should peacefully settle down in the faith. But, seeing too much to deny and not enough to affirm, I am in a pitiful state, where I have wished a

hundred times over that, if there is a God supporting nature, she should unequivocally proclaim him, and that, if the signs in nature are deceptive, they should be completely erased; that nature should say all or nothing, so that I could see what course I ought to follow.[15]

Indeed, the message from nature seems shrouded in uncertainty and mystery, even though the evidence of divine footprints seems "too much to deny." One of my favorite verbal paintings comes from theologian Barbara Brown Taylor, who posits a more appealing way of viewing such subtle indicators of a design presence:

The universe has a memory that predates the Big Bang. Back before that explosion sent energy racing every which way at speeds faster than light, there was the egg of the universe in which all places were one place and all things were one thing. . . .

Mind, matter and time were not different yet. They were all floating in the same yolk. Then the universe was born and the one became many. Quantum particles became planets, galaxies, clusters and superclusters. Atoms became blue-green algae, toads, palm trees and swans. Space became here or there, as time became then or now. But deep down in the being of these things remains the memory of their being one, which makes them behave in ways that torture scientists. Space and time are not separable. Light is both particle and wave. A particle way over there responds instantly to a particle way over here, as if each could read the other's mind. . . .

Where is God in this picture? All over the place. Up there down here. Inside my skin and out. God is the web, the energy, the space, the light— not captured in them, as if any of those concepts were more real than what unites them, but revealed in that singular, vast net of relationship that animates everything that is. . . . When the fog finally clears, we shall know there is only One.[16]

Let's now turn to a more personal place to look for evidence of divine footprints in the cosmos: some universal characteristics of human nature that have provocative and profound implications for the possibility that God exists.

4

WHO ARE WE?

Asking *Who are we?* takes the search for divine footprints to the most personal level: that of self-understanding. What does it mean to be human? If the universe suggests that we are meant to be here, then what does human nature suggest about a possible Creator?

There are many aspects of human nature that we might point to as indicators of a divine creative intent: creativity, self-consciousness, volition and so forth. But I want to zero in on two fundamental characteristics that seem to be at the most primal level of human thought and behavior, and least likely to be explained satisfactorily by accidental biology and evolutionary adaptation alone: (1) moral conscience, and (2) the drive toward relationship.

WHY DO WE KNOW RIGHT FROM WRONG?

German philosopher Immanuel Kant wrote, "Two things fill the mind with ever new and increasing wonder and awe, the more often and the more intensely reflection concentrates upon them: the starry heaven above me and the moral law within me."[1]

Today, we don't bring up this "moral law" very often as evidence for the existence of God, possibly because it is so fraught with potential conflict over defining what is or isn't moral. However, I am not as interested in specific moral codes per se as I am in the fact that we even have moral inclinations at all. Indeed, our so-called sense of right and wrong is a more common part of our everyday thinking and expression than the physical laws of nature.

Think for a moment about how often we invoke moral law in our everyday lives. We may not call it that, but we often say things like, "That just isn't right," or "I can't do that in good conscience," or "It isn't fair." (Kids may put it in more personal terms such as, "If you do that I'm going to tell Mom," or "Please don't tell the teacher.") When we say those kinds of things, we are subconsciously but definitely appealing to some higher principle that we assume is self-evident.

Where does this kind of standard or principle or law come from? Religious people might readily cite the Ten Commandments, the Golden Rule or other teachings from sacred texts as the source of their certainty about these matters—meaning that these rules come ultimately from God. But nonreligious people are also likely to believe in right and wrong—meaning that they too believe in some kind of morality built into the very essence of our human nature. But they would say there are explanations that do not need a God for authentication.

The most common alternative explanation to God for the widespread belief in and use of certain moral principles is the process of social evolution. Simply put, this explanation says that the various principles of morality we use in our daily lives have been developed over time out of the lessons learned from living—rules that help us better live together. It is a kind of moral evolution that has selected what works and what doesn't for human community and advance-ment. As we have developed these rules, often through painful mis-takes and social experiments, we have reduced them to moral codes and regulations that we can teach to each new generation.

This explanation can even allow for the religious support of some of these societal rules or expectations, that is, religious leaders and teachers who use the name of God to explain the rules' origin or give them more authority. But such explanations don't definitively prove that there actually is a God who created this kind of moral order. Kant himself didn't believe that morality proved the existence of God, but he did acknowledge that such belief helped to buttress morality.

I confess that I find the use of the existence of moral law as an argument for the existence of God less compelling than the exis-tence of the remarkable physical universe described in previous chapters. Put another way, once living creatures had arrived at the point that allowed more sophisticated thinking and communica-tion, it seems more likely that moral law could have developed out of trial-and-error experience than that the physical universe could have developed by accident. But of course that begs the question of how living creatures reached the stage where they *could* develop thinking and communication. And if I believe that could only hap-pen because of the mind of God, then I'm really saying that God is also ultimately the author of moral law, because the possibility of such law is also a part of the cards dealt at creation. This argument has been used by many theologians over the years and was devel-oped in delightful fashion by the great Christian writer of the mid-twentieth century, C. S. Lewis (see bibliography).

However, there is a more sophisticated argument in favor of morality as an independent reality versus the product of social learning. And that argument goes something like this: It is true that much of what we call moral law seems to be a commonsense description of what it takes to make society work well. If we murder, lie and steal, society clearly pays a price, so it is better for society as a whole and us as individuals if we don't do such things. But what about the kind of morality that may be better for society as a whole but not necessarily for the individual, at least not at the moment. For example, what about the immediate impulse to rescue someone from a burning building? Clearly that impulse might be good for the person in the building, but it might also put the rescuer at great risk.

To rephrase the question, what is the source of morality that impels action potentially fatal to the individual but nonetheless seems like the "right" thing to do? Is there a kind of morality that really can't be explained by the evolution of societal rules so much as by a created conviction that something is right no matter the personal consequences? And if so, where does that kind of morality come from?

I am not saying that such a kind of "inner light" definitively proves the existence of God—not at all. But it raises the interesting question of how to explain the phenomenon we all have experienced—the willingness to at least think about doing something we believe is right even though it is not beneficial or popular or helpful to our own comfort or safety.

WHY ARE WE SO RELATIONALLY DRIVEN?

When Randy Thornhill and Craig Palmer published *A Natural History of Rape*, contending that rape is an evolutionary strategy for maximizing male reproductive success, they ignited a firestorm of protest (as well as criticism of their methodology, it should be noted).[2] Few debates can cast feminists and religious fundamentalists on the same side of an issue, but this one did. The theory that rape confers evolutionary advantage cuts precisely to the very core of debate over human nature. How are *good* and *bad* defined—by Darwinian standards of what accrues to the benefit of the human species, or by moral values?

A corollary to this central question is how we perceive the issue of marriage and marital fidelity. Why are humans inclined to forge lifelong, monogamous commitments—for procreation and family survival, or because a desire for intimate relationship is built into human nature, and such relationships are essential for inner growth?

Clearly, both humans and animals create family bonds to perpetuate the species and provide survival strategies. This behavior is easily attributable to the dynamics of natural selection. But the furor over Thornhill and Palmer's thesis suggests that we instinctively attach moral values to sexuality, over and above reproduction and survival issues. Our mating behavior is sufficiently distinctive from animals' that anyone would be hard-pressed to explain it convincingly *only* in terms of evolutionary strategy.

In practical experience human sexuality is bound up with our deepest needs and longings. We view it as a primal dimension of intimate relationship with a partner, not simply a physical need to be gratified at will. When sex is isolated from this matrix of relationships and marginalized to the level of physical gratification alone, we tend to consign it to a category specifically defined by its preoccupation with the act itself: pornography, prostitution, exploitation, adul-

tery—or a fantasy utopia of sexual indulgence without consequences. Regardless of religious convictions, we seem to have a
built-in sense that sex naturally belongs within the framework of nur-
turing, life-giving relationships.

This drive for relationship, not just for sex, is a universal characteristic of human nature. We spend much of our lives consumed
with desire for an intimate relationship that will satisfy all our needs,
emotional as well as physical. If we are not anticipating something
we don't have, we are critiquing what we do have. If we have lost a
relationship through betrayal or conflict, it costs us enormous energy
in anger and sadness. If the relationship has been ripped away from
us by violence or death, we face debilitating grief and the difficult
challenge of recovery. Many of us define our quality of life based on
whether we have a fulfilling, intimate relationship with a partner.

Why is this? One way to view it is as evidence of our moral conscience, which we have already touched on. But another explanation is that we are innately designed for intimate connection. Those
who live isolated lives are the exception to typical human practice.
We know that physical touch has extraordinary power to increase
well-being, and the lack of it jeopardizes well-being. Studies show
that happily married couples enjoy better health and longer lives
than singles or unhappily married individuals. Our family relationships are designed to prepare us for such adult attachments—albeit
in actual practice they can sometimes sabotage as much as nurture
our ability to build and sustain them.

Much of our drive toward human relationships might conceivably be explained as complex sociological phenomena, which developed along with the increasingly complex demands of growing pop-

ulations and the interactions of diverse societies and cultures. But this clearly cuts against the grain of our daily, lived experience in which relationships provide a sense of meaning and purpose of a vastly different order than survival needs of food and shelter.

This relational drive manifests itself not just in a horizontal dimension but in a vertical one as well—even more suggestive of a divine source. Virtually all religions and mythologies share a common sense that human beings are in relationship to someone or something suprahuman. It can be argued that religions and mythologies have developed *because* humans need a way of systematizing and managing their relationship to the transcendent, but that says nothing about whether a transcendent being exists. Philosopher Rudolf Otto calls this perceived transcendence the "numinous" and our sense of relationship to it as "creature-consciousness," observing that it recurs in all forms of mystical experience as "the consciousness of the littleness of every creature in face of that which is above all creatures."[3]

If there is no other reality than the material world, no other being than human beings and animals, then why is this sense of relationship to a transcendent force or entity so persistent? This sense is heightened for some by indications from brain researchers that we are, in casual terms, "hard-wired for God"—that is, the suggestion that there might be a neurological basis for spiritual experience. Drs. Eugene d'Aquili and Andrew Newberg, for example, conducted brain-imaging studies of adults involved in spiritual activities such as meditation or prayer and found an increased activity in specific areas such as the prefrontal cortex, the front area of the thinking part of our brain. They state that such experiences "are based in observable functions of the brain" and that such spiritual practices are "genu-ine, neurobiological events."[4]

This research is cited in the very readable report "Hardwired to Connect," which was released in the fall of 2003. The report focuses on the biological need for spirituality in children and adolescents. The Commission on Children at Risk cosponsored this report with the YMCA, Dartmouth Medical School and the Institute for American Values. The Commission consists of thirty-three children's doctors, research scientists and mental health and youth service professionals. It includes such luminaries as T. Berry Brazelton, Robert Coles and Alvin Poussaint of Harvard Medical School. I found this report to be so provocative that I would urge you to get a copy for yourself by contacting the Institute for American Values. (Their website can be found at <www.americanvalues.org>.) Here, I will simply quote excerpts from the report to give you a sense of its content and conclusions:

> Much of the first half of this report is a presentation of scientific evidence . . . showing that the human child is "hardwired to connect." We are hardwired for other people and for moral meaning and openness to the transcendent. Meeting these basic needs for connection is essential to health and to human flourishing.
>
> For what may be the first time, a diverse group of scientists and other experts on children's health is publicly recommending that our society pay considerably more attention to young people's moral, spiritual, and religious needs.
>
> Primary nurturing relationships influence early spiritual development, and spiritual development can influence us biologically in the same ways that primary nurturing relationships do. The human brain appears to be organized to ask ultimate questions and seek ultimate answers.

> In short, the two kinds of connectedness analyzed in this report—connection to others and connection to the transcendent—seem to influence the same biological systems in quite similar ways. This phenomenon may help explain why some people find, in their religious faith and spiritual practice, some of the very sources of security and well-being that were not available to them from their parents.[5]

In an age when we are more attuned than ever to the terrible cost of broken relationships and of violence between persons, ethnic groups and nations, it is worth considering that we might have a common ground for human relationships that transcends all such divisions. The suggestion of a divine presence that has created us for relationship with itself and with one another offers hope of finding both authentic personal wholeness and social peace.

TRACKING DIVINE FOOTPRINTS?

In the course of my work on this book, a friend wrote in response to some of my early material:

> In your schema, God is regarded as a probability that seems irresistible, given the synchronizing complexities of physics and biology that result in our being here at this time. . . . okay. If one accepts this, as one might, God is what we call the unfathomable "x" responsible for the design/implementation. X need not have any anthropomorphic attributes; there is no reason to require any of religion's traditional reverential qualities: love, mercy, etc. . . . In short, God does not emerge as the traditional one of religion.[6]

My friend is entirely correct. At this point I have not made any case for the more personal God traditionally associated with Judeo-Christian religious belief. And, in fact, I will never be able to make a traditionally scientific case for a connection between the "God of creation" and the "God of religion." However, it would seem strange (even illogical?) if the God who created a universe apparently designed to result in human beings who think and feel and communicate did not also attempt to reach out to such creatures with many different kinds of communication, including inspired Scriptures and perceptive prophets. And in the next two sections I will be suggesting that the God of creation I have been pointing to in this section has done just that—tried to reach us and teach us through human channels that would not overwhelm our freedom to choose but would offer guidance about how we might best live in tune with our world.

Another friend challenged my assumption that God should be available and knowable to everyone: "Is God as knowable to a poor woman dying from AIDS in Sudan as God is to you?" he wrote. "Is God as knowable to the sneaker factory worker who never finished high school and doesn't know the basics of high school biology?" The quick answer to both questions would appear to be an easy no. I have education and means to observe and contemplate the mysteries of the universe and the human body—and thanks to comfortable circumstances, the time to do so—that others clearly lack.

But to say that God is therefore *not* as knowable to the Sudan sufferer or the factory worker might also be a presumptuous answer. For example, the psalmist of Hebrew Scripture is able to write eloquently that "the heavens declare the glory of God" and that "the skies proclaim the work of his hands" without any understanding of modern cosmology. In less elegant ways, might not the poor woman in Sudan and the factory worker who does not understand high school biology have a sense of awe regarding the forces of nature that could be just as meaningful to them as the more sophisticated arguments are for others? Certainly it would seem unfair if God could be known only through reason, since that would obviously give advantage to those with greater intellectual resources. And for me, a God who is unfair is not the kind of God I could respect, let alone worship.

In conclusion, I do believe there are "footprints" of an intelligence in our universe that expresses itself in the mind-boggling complexity and "coincidences" of our cosmos and in the very nature of what it means to be human—the conscience that so often calls us to do the unpopular or unexpected, the intense bonds of relationship that shape and direct our lives. But as my friend observed, these kinds of footprints are a long way from the claims of traditional Judeo-Christian religion for the existence of a personal God. Those claims come largely from Scriptures and the religious traditions out of which they have come—and it is to these sources that I now turn.

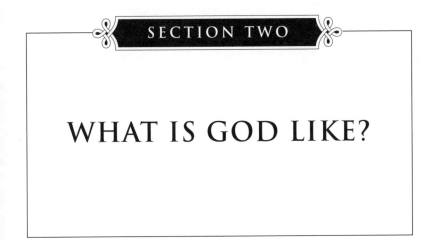

SECTION TWO

WHAT IS GOD LIKE?

5

Why Bother with Religion and the Bible?

✦

So far I have presented paths of understanding God as Creator from the natural world. But we are still left with the question, *How do we find out what this creator God is like?* This leads us to the issue of organized religion, which typically poses a system of answers to such questions.

Religion can turn people away as easily as it invites them. By stressing dogmatic answers, it can shut down legitimate questions. By claiming exclusive truth, it can breed arrogance. By superficially categorizing mystery, it can attempt to control it and claim exclusive access to it, wielding it as power over others.

Religion too often breeds conflict, from the bombast of street preachers screaming condemnation to the tragic violence of religious wars. Major traditions—Christian, Islamic, Jewish, Buddhist, Hindu—create dividing lines of hate around the world, from Northern Ireland to the Middle East to India and Sri Lanka. And often these traditions can't even prevent their own adherents from deadly power struggles, such as Protestants and Catholics in Northern Ireland or Shiites and Sunnis in the Middle East.

Why bother with it at all?

To make the case *for* religion, at its best, we can view it as a vehicle through which spiritual truth is communicated, interpreted and applied. Most religions offer some version of "Thus saith the Lord," along with explanations of what the divinely revealed sayings mean and how they guide the thought and behavior of followers. Organized religion also provides the important dimension of community—a place to process our spiritual search, to share it and find both challenge and encouragement, a lifelong group of people with whom to travel through this earthly journey in some common commitment to God and one another.

Those who avoid or reject religion entirely yet remain spiritual searchers often speak of discovering the truth within, the God within you, the divine self who is one with all other individual selves and with the cosmic force or energy or consciousness uniting them. I have chosen a path of belief that depends on a God above and beyond myself, a story that involves me but does not begin and end with me. And for me, that path of belief has been distinctly shaped by the stories recorded in the Bible produced by the Judeo-Christian tradition.

THE BIBLE TELLS ME SO

In my childhood, pondering the starry heaven above went hand in hand with listening in rapt attention to stories from the Bible. In Sunday school classes and my mother's nightly readings to me, I was enthralled by the stories of God's mighty works and wonders as recorded in the Old Testament. And I was totally captivated by the stories about Jesus. I had no doubt that the two of them (God and Jesus) were in heaven, looking down on me as their special child. Do I smile at this childlike faith now that I am so much more informed and "sophisticated" about the Bible—how it was written, what it means, what we should believe about its stories? I won't give you my answer just yet. I must first lead you through an exploration of what I believe we should know about the Bible today.

The Bible is not a single book but a collection of very different kinds of minibooks written during a span of roughly a thousand years of dynamic and changing human history. (Indeed, the word *Bible* is derived from the Greek word *biblia*, meaning "books.") Before the content of the Bible was written, it was spoken aloud in community. Storytelling conveyed the content from one generation to the next. Even after the earliest Scriptures were written down, they were still read aloud because not everyone had access to the texts or the ability to read them. And there are no original manuscripts by the original writers in the original languages for any of these texts—only copies (some very old) that have come through various religious traditions.

Another complicating factor is that many people treat the Bible as if it fell out of the sky from heaven, intact. "God said it, I believe it!" shows up on bumper stickers. People can say all kinds of things and claim "that's what the Bible says," as if it came straight from God with absolute clarity. Most Christians, however, have a more complicated understanding of their Bible.

The Bible is the central guide for Christian faith, although various streams of Christianity differ on how to interpret and apply its authority for belief and practice; unfortunately, some extreme groups use the Bible abusively in the name of God. Some people stay away from the Bible because it is confusing or has been used as a weapon to enforce doctrine or manipulate others according to agendas we impose on it. Because I believe it is important to read the Bible for ourselves and make our own decisions about it, I believe it helps to know what the Bible actually is, how it came about and why there is such controversy over certain issues. I will try to give you a very simplified version, but if you want more detailed accounts, check "Suggested Reading" for recommendations.

The Hebrew Bible. The Hebrew Bible is sometimes also called the *Tanakh*, an acronym for the following three words that describe the three main sections of the Jewish Bible:

- *Torah* (or "instruction," comprising five books also often known as the books of the Law, the books of Moses or the Pentateuch).

- *Nevi'im* (or "prophets," comprising eight books of Israel's history and the books Christians usually call the Prophets).

- *Kethuvim* (or "writings," comprising eleven books of poetry, wisdom and further histories)

Though ordered and numbered differently, these twenty-four books are the same as the Protestant Bible's thirty-nine Old Testament books. (Roman Catholic and Orthodox Bibles contain a few additional books or parts of books predating the New Testament.)

The earliest written forms of these books are dated to approximately three thousand years ago, and they are based on a prior oral transmission spread over roughly one thousand years. The oldest of these books, the first five, are often referred to as the "books of Moses" because of the ancient and still widely held belief that they were written by Moses. However, modern scholarship suggests that they were formed into written documents over a six-hundred-year period beginning around 1000 B.C., though many acknowledge that some original sources could go back to Moses.

Although debate among scholars continues, many believe that the written form of the first five books came from various sources that have different themes or identifying characteristics. Others have noted variable versions of the same story (such as two separate creation stories in Genesis that do not agree in some details) and different names for God, which point to more than a single author. As to the rest of the books of the Hebrew Scriptures, their content was transmitted orally for generations and was probably not finalized in present written form until about 400 B.C. However, it took another five hundred years until Jewish religious leaders finally agreed on an official list of the books that would become the present Jewish Bible—which was about the same time the books of the Christian "New" Testament were first being written.

The books that would eventually become the New Testament of the Christian Bible were written during the last half of the first century, within a generation or two after the death of Jesus. (I will deal much more with the New Testament later in this section as I deal with the life and teachings of Jesus.) These books circulated as individual manuscripts within the early church for many decades, but they were not accepted as the official canon of the Christian church until almost three hundred years later when prominent church leaders of the time gave their blessing to the list.

The Bible in Greek, Latin, German and English. By the third century before the time of Jesus, the Jewish people had become so much a part of Greek culture that Jewish leaders became concerned that their Scriptures would no longer be widely understood in Hebrew. So they developed a translation from Hebrew into Greek that eventually became the most popular form of the Jewish Bible. (It is widely known today as the Septuagint—which means "seventy"— because of legend that the first five books were translated by seventy-two Jewish elders in seventy-two days—and seventy-two can be rounded off to seventy if you are not too fussy about numbers.) And even though Jesus spoke Aramaic, a Semitic language related to Hebrew, the New Testament writers also wrote in Greek because it was the common language of the people they were addressing and because the Greek Septuagint was the Jewish Scripture often used by them in their worship.

At that same time, about three centuries after Jesus, a priest named Jerome, working for twenty years in Bethlehem, translated the Jewish Bible and the New Testament into Latin because it was the language of the Roman Empire, which now had made Christianity its official religion. (Jerome also decided to use the name *Jesus*, which was how the Greek New Testament writers had translated the Hebrew name *Joshua*, or *Yeshua*, which was probably Jesus' actual name.) Jerome's version became known as the Vulgate Bible, based on the ancient meaning of that word, which was not "vulgar" in today's negative sense but more accurately translated then as "common."

However, this Vulgate Bible was hardly common among ordinary people; it was still being copied by hand—meaning that only priests and the wealthy could actually get it and read it for themselves. And even when the famous Gutenberg printing press became operational in A.D. 1450, less than two hundred copies of the Bible were produced—all in Latin.

In the early 1500s, Martin Luther translated the Bible into German—much to the consternation of the Roman Catholic Church, which did not believe the masses could actually understand the Bible by themselves. And when William Tyndale of England wanted to translate the New Testament into English, he had to go to Germany to do so. Even so, he was captured, tried for heresy, then strangled and burned at the stake for his efforts. Ironically, his work became the basis for the famous King James Version in 1611, and the rest is truly history. Today there are more than 3,000 versions of the Bible in English alone. It is available in more than 40 European languages, 125 Asian languages, more than 100 African languages and at least 15 Native American languages.

I believe this history indicates that whatever else the Bible is (and I will be dealing with the "whatever else" in the rest of this section), it is also a human book, written down over hundreds of years by many different writers and editors. Nonetheless, this amazingly diverse collection of writings has inspired countless readers through the centuries to believe in the God described in its pages. Indeed, there clearly is a unifying theme among the many writers of the Bible, namely, the belief that they were writing about God's interaction with human history in general and often with them in particular. Not surprisingly, their writings are representative of the culture and history of the times in which they were actually written (often considerably later than the events they are describing). That means, in my view, that while we must take the overall themes of Scripture very seriously, we must also be very careful not to take particular passages out of the context of their time and use them as "proof texts" to support or attack particular views in our time. As others have said, we ought not use Scripture as a drunk uses a lamppost—for support rather than for illumination.

I must speak in personal terms at this point. While I deeply revere the Bible (including both the Hebrew Scriptures and the New Testament) as an inspired record of God's truth in changing historical circumstances, I do not believe that the biblical record is primarily intended to provide a detailed blueprint of exactly how we should live today. In fact, almost all who honor the Bible engage in some selectivity—ignoring detailed advice about daily living that is restricted to certain people contemporary with the biblical writers but trying to discern the principles behind such advice that might be freshly applied to modern life. Unfortunately, some religious leaders today still use selected biblical passages clearly tied to past cultural beliefs or some specific circumstances of biblical times as normative for today's world—using them as support for particular personal biases rather than taking the time to discover the underlying universal themes of Scripture that would override particular historical practices.

For example, opponents of allowing women to serve as full ministers or priests in the church often cite a passage from the apostle Paul in his letter to the church at Corinth:

> Women should remain silent in the churches. They are not allowed to speak, but must be in submission, as the Law says. If they want to inquire about something, they should ask their own husbands at home; for it is disgraceful for a woman to speak in the church. (1 Corinthians 14:34-35, New International Version)

Today, most scholars assume that Paul was speaking to a very specific problem in which some women were disrupting worship with their insistence on speaking out of turn. Indeed, in this very same letter Paul clearly assumes that women pray in the church, and in other writings he clearly acknowledges the important role of women in church affairs. And even more important for me is the attitude of Jesus toward women as recorded in the Gospels, which was clearly one of appreciation and respect, far more so than the general attitude of his time.

So while isolated passages of the Bible may speak to a specific situation in biblical times, the clear overall theme of Jesus' life and teaching can be quite different. Indeed, for me the most important "universal themes" of Scripture come from the life and teachings of Jesus. And for me that life and those teachings become the key to understanding the rest of the Bible.

WHAT THE BIBLE SAYS ABOUT JESUS

I will now focus on the story of Jesus of Nazareth rather than begin with the spiritually inspiring history of the people of Israel as recorded in the Hebrew Scriptures. I do this for two reasons. First, my own history, as I have already indicated, is steeped in the Christian church and its teachings; I want to stick to what I know best and what I most need to wrestle with in this attempt to account for my present faith. Second, as a corollary, I feel far less competent to comment on Jewish history, even though I honor it and deeply believe that the God of Israel is the same God that Christians worship.

Indeed, there would be no Christian faith were it not for the faith of the Jews, who have taught us all to consider the God who, in the words of the prophet Micah, asks us to "act justly, to love mercy and to walk humbly." And I believe that Jesus was a deeply pious Jew who would be appalled by what some so-called Christians have sometimes done to Jews—including, of course, some Christians who participated in the truly horrific Holocaust. But I will let others guide those of you who wish to study the faith journey of the people of Israel as described in the Hebrew Scriptures, which became the "Old" Testament of the Christian Bible.

However, I do want to call special attention to a remarkable writer, Thomas Cahill. In his book *The Gifts of the Jews* Cahill describes the religious history of the Jews and the content of the Hebrew Scriptures with a unique combination of poetic insight and scholarly perceptiveness. His penetrating analysis of the dramatic change in human history wrought by the Jewish faith in one God is marked by both beauty and brevity. He comes to this stirring conclusion about the consistent message to be found in Hebrew Scripture:

> The Jews gave us a whole new vocabulary, a whole new Temple of the Spirit, an inner landscape of ideas and feelings that had never been known before. Over many centuries of trauma and suffering they came to believe in one God, the Creator of the universe, whose meaning underlies all his creation and who enters human history to bring his purposes to pass. Because of their unique belief—monotheism—the Jews were able to give us the Great Whole, a unified universe that makes sense and that, because of its evident superiority as a worldview, completely overwhelms the warring and contradictory phenomena of polytheism. They gave us the Conscience of the West, the belief that this God who is One is not the God of outward show but the "still, small voice" of conscience, the God of compassion, the God who "will be there," the God who cares about each of his creatures, especially the human beings he created "in his own image," and that he insists we do the same.[1]

It is against the background of this wondrous story of the formation of Jewish monotheism that I now look at the story of a Jewish man who both challenged and reformulated the faith into which he was born.

The record of what Jesus said. I must tell you up front that I have been both fascinated and frustrated by the many scholarly (and not so scholarly) writings of the past several decades attempting to sort out the "Jesus of history" from the "Christ of faith"—that is, attempting to determine what we can really know as the "historical truth" about the life of Jesus—versus how the early Jesus Movement might have presented the accounts of his life when they eventually wrote them down. My frustration with these writers stems from their incredibly diverse conclusions even though they are using the same basic information. They all read the same material—and each other's writings—and yet come to very different conclusions about much of it. (The most publicized of these efforts is the Jesus Seminar, a group of self-organized experts started in 1985. However, the Jesus Seminar itself is not connected with any academic center or scholarly society and its conclusions have often been criticized by many mainstream biblical scholars.) It is way beyond the scope of this book to attempt an assessment of such efforts, but I would refer you to my "Suggested Reading" list for some examples of these writings.

Ultimately, almost everything we know about the actual life and teachings of Jesus comes from the New Testament, especially the four Gospels. However, there are some very brief but intriguing references to Jesus and the early Jesus movement in "outside" sources (that is, writings that are not from the believing community that produced the New Testament). In fact there are about twenty such fragmentary references in existence, and I will briefly list some of these as described by Luke Timothy Johnson (no relation) in his scholarly but readable book titled *The Real Jesus*. (The quotes in the following paragraphs are from the Johnson book.)

Most intriguing are some references in the writings of Josephus, a Jew (Joseph ben Matthias) who was befriended by the Romans in the first century and wrote an account of the Jewish people under his new Roman name. Josephus makes three brief references in his *Antiquities of the Jews*, written toward the end of that century. In one he mentions John the Baptist, in another he mentions James as "the brother of Jesus who was called the Christ" and in the most extensive comment he writes:

> At this time there appeared Jesus, a wise man, *if indeed one should call him a man*. For he was a doer of startling deeds, a teacher of people who receive the truth with pleasure. And he gained a following both among many Jews and among many of Greek origin. *He was the Messiah*. And when Pilate, because of an accusation made by the leading men among us, condemned him to the cross, those who had loved him previously did not cease to do so. *For he appeared to them on the third day, living again, just as the divine prophets had spoken of these and countless other wondrous things about him*. And up until this very day the tribe of Christians, named after him, has not died out.[2] (Italics are added to indicate a rather broad scholarly consensus that these words were added by later editors favorable to the early Christian community.)

There are some references to Jesus in other Jewish sources such as the Babylonian Talmud, but they come from a later period and are colored by the bitter rivalry of that period between the Jesus Movement and rabbinical Judaism. There are also some second-century references by Roman writers. These brief accounts shed very little light on the life of Jesus, though they do confirm awareness of Jesus and his followers in very early references other than the New Testament. But it is to the four Gospels of the New Testament that we must turn for very detailed accounts of the life and teachings of the Jew who became such a monumental turning point in human spiritual history.

As is the case with the books of the Hebrew Scriptures, there are no original manuscripts of the New Testament in existence. However, there are over five thousand very old copies of various parts of the New Testament, far more than for other ancient writings of the same period. The actual writing of the Gospels was undoubtedly based in large part on oral transmissions, the common way of preserving history and stories in ancient cultures—before printing and computers made that task much easier! Therefore, stories about Jesus, his teachings and his life, were probably memorized much as we might memorize passages of a play for performance. Those stories could then be passed on as sacred tradition from one generation to the next.[3]

All of which is to say that even though the actual writing of the Gospels occurred several decades after the death of Jesus, I have come to believe they are a reliable guide to what Jesus actually did and said. Clearly they are not biographies in the modern style. For example, they say almost nothing about his childhood and young-adult years, and they leave out the kind of detail about his relationship with friends and family that so permeate modern biographical writing. Rather, I see them as an attempt to selectively summarize the three years of his public ministry starting at age thirty, during which he lived and taught in a truly revolutionary manner.

The Gospel accounts. Each of the four Gospels is constructed using somewhat different literary styles and with specific goals and target audiences in mind. Here is a brief look at each in the order they were probably written during the second half of the first century. (The exact dates of the initial writing of these Gospels is a matter of considerable scholarly dispute, but there is a wide consensus that they were all written during the second half of the first century—that is, within twenty to seventy years after the death of Jesus.)

THE GOSPEL ACCORDING TO MARK (written approximately A.D. 60-70?). Though not one of the twelve original disciples of Jesus, a person named John Mark is mentioned in the New Testament and he may be the author of this Gospel. It is the shortest of the Gospels and widely felt to be the first to be written, even though it was placed second in the New Testament order by the early Christians. Many scholars believe that Matthew and Luke had Mark's Gospel in hand when they wrote their accounts and they used a considerable amount of Mark's material in their own Gospel accounts. Mark strongly emphasized the theme of Jesus as a "suffering servant," obedient to the call of God in service to others, a theme found in all the other Gospels.

THE GOSPEL ACCORDING TO MATTHEW (written approximately A.D. 70-80?). The writing of this Gospel is usually attributed to the same Matthew identified in the Gospels as the tax collector called by Jesus as one of his twelve disciples. According to most scholars Matthew was writing especially for a Jewish audience, attempting to convince them that Jesus is the long-awaited Messiah by making reference to prophecies from the Hebrew Scriptures. The early church thought his was the first Gospel written and therefore placed it first in the New Testament.

THE GOSPEL ACCORDING TO LUKE (written approximately A.D. 80-90?). Written in more elegant Greek than either Matthew or Mark, this Gospel is believed to have been written by the same Luke who traveled with the apostle Paul in his missionary journeys (see p. 91) and is described in one of his letters as "the beloved physician." Luke's Gospel is especially trying to reach out to the Gentile (non-Jewish) population of the first century, not surprising since he was apparently a Gentile himself.

THE GOSPEL ACCORDING TO JOHN (written approximately A.D. 90-100?). This Gospel, traditionally believed to be written by the "beloved apostle" John, is very different in style and considerably different in content than the first three Gospels—which are referred to as the Synoptic Gospels ("viewed together") because they are so similar in their style and content. John leaves out the stories of Jesus' birth, temptation in the wilderness and agony in the Garden of Gethsemane. He includes unique miracle stories such as the changing of water into wine and the raising of Lazarus from the dead. He does not include the penetrating parables so characteristic of the first three Gospels but instead presents long blocks of monologues by Jesus. John's Gospel includes more of the theological language characteristic of the Jesus Movement in the later part of the first century.

Given the fact that these Gospels (from the Greek for "good news") were written by different authors over different time periods and based in part on different oral and written sources, I don't find it at all surprising that they differ with each other in the ordering of events, various details and selection of content. (Remember, even with modern communication technology such as video and eyewitness reports, events such as the death of President Kennedy can lead to very different reports from different observers.) Indeed, I would argue that these differences support authenticity—that there was obviously no conspiracy among the Gospel writers to "get their stories straight" before writing them down. For example, Luke and Matthew have extensive birth stories that place Jesus' birth in the town of Bethlehem. Mark and John say nothing about his birth or Bethlehem and start their Gospel accounts with Jesus living in Nazareth. Another example: the beautiful parables of the Good Samaritan and the Prodigal Son are found only in the Gospel of Luke, which is not surprising given that their emphasis on the love of God reaching out to all people would be very appealing to Gentiles, the primary group for whom Luke is probably writing.

But if you were to sit down and read the four Gospels in parallel—with similar material side by side—you would realize just how much these Gospels have in common. In another remarkable book, *Desire of the Everlasting Hills: The World Before and After Jesus,* Thomas Cahill summarizes the different accounts of Jesus in the four Gospels of the New Testament with this observation:

> In nothing is their unity so evident as in their portrayal of Jesus. Though he is presented in various lights and shadows, depending on the concerns, personality, and skill of each author, he exudes even under this treatment a remarkable consistency, so that we feel on finishing this story, whether it is told well or badly, simply or extravagantly, that we know the man— and that in each telling he is identifiably the same man. This phenomenon

of consistency beneath the differences makes Jesus a unique figure in world literature: never have so many writers managed to convey the same impression of the same human being over and over again. More than this, Jesus—what he says, what he does—is almost always comprehensible to the reader, who needs no introduction, no scholarly background, to penetrate the meaning of Jesus' words and actions."[4]

I would add my own personal affirmation of this conclusion by Cahill. Unlike most writings about historical figures of the same general period, there is an intuitive and immediate connection with most of the material in the Gospel accounts of the life and teachings of Jesus. His parables and life experiences often speak to universal questions and longings that transcend the particular concerns of his own time. Most anyone can read the Gospels and feel that they speak to the same human condition we wrestle with today!

The letters of the apostle Paul (dated approximately A.D. 50-70). Actually, the earliest written books of the New Testament are not any of the Gospels but the varied letters of the person known as the apostle Paul whose brief "biography" appears in the book of Acts, the fifth book in the New Testament, also apparently written by Luke. This book picks up the story of the followers of Jesus after his death and resurrection as reported in the Gospels. Chapter nine of the book of Acts tells the famous story of the calling of Saul, the Jew who was persecuting followers of Jesus, to become a follower of Jesus. (He was renamed Paul.) This newly converted "apostle Paul" then became an indefatigable traveler throughout the Middle East and Europe. He was also a prolific writer of letters to some of the churches he founded and some of the individuals he met during those journeys. And while the letters contain much personal material and practical advice, some of it difficult to understand today especially as it relates to sexual practice and the role of women in the church, they also contain some of the most elegant and sophisticated theological material to be found in the New Testament. But pertinent to my discussion about the historical reliability of the Gospel accounts of the life of Jesus, these letters also make many references to Jesus that concur with the somewhat later Gospel accounts. In other words, these earliest of the New Testament writings, written only a generation after Jesus' death (when some eyewitnesses were presumably still alive), already reference the life of Jesus in a manner consistent with the Gospel accounts written later.

Other recently discovered sources. Many of you have heard about the Dead Sea Scrolls found in Israel and the library of ancient manuscripts found at Nag Hammadi, a town in east-central Egypt. Actually, the vast majority of scholars now believe that the Dead Sea Scrolls do not shed any significant new light on Jesus but rather describe the thinking and practices of a particular Jewish sect (the so-called Qumran community) as it existed during the first century. However, there has been considerable interest on the part of some Jesus scholars in the thirteen leather-bound books that were found accidentally by an Egyptian peasant in 1945 when he was digging near Nag Hammadi. They were eventually determined to be the writings of Gnostics, an early Christian sect that held very different views from those of most others in the Jesus movement of that time. For example, they denied that Jesus was ever a real physical human being and therefore denied the bodily resurrection as a real event. They emphasized spirituality as an inner journey to discover secret knowledge not easily available to others. Even though this material is of great interest to scholars, my own conclusion after reading many debates about it is that it does not add substantively to the basic portrait we have of Jesus from the four canonical Gospels. It is to those sources I now turn.[5]

6

WHAT DID JESUS TEACH?

How can people reading the same Bible come up with understandings that differ as radically as a far-right fundamentalist preacher versus a left-wing social-action advocate? Too often passages from the Gospels have been quoted or misquoted to justify personal agendas in a way that turns people away from reading for themselves what Jesus actually taught.

Aware of my own possible biases, and having read the Gospels many times before but always in bits and pieces, I decided to read the four Gospels straight through over a two-day period rather than getting bogged down in specific passages. I used a harmony edition, which places similar passages from the four Gospels side by side for comparison. My goal was to approach the texts as a reporter reading them for the first time, quickly recording initial impressions before the bias filter took over.

Is it possible for someone with my background, who has read many books about the life and teachings of Jesus, to read the Gospels as if for the first time and present unbiased impressions? I have given it an honest try, using my training as a scientist and reporter to record facts and impressions in an objective manner. I am not arguing that the Gospels can be taken as journalistic recordings similar to videotape on the evening news, but I do think it's possible to sit down and simply read through the Gospels to gain very useful overall impressions.

Before you can judge my effort, you will need to read the Gospels yourself—all the way through as I did. You can't, anymore than I could, rely on your past impressions or readings or beliefs. For those of you who read them for the first time, this should be relatively easy. For those of you who have read and heard them through the years, the task will be more difficult. However, if you do it openly and honestly, it might be as surprising for you as it was for me. In fact, I suggest that much of what Christians argue about among themselves often has little to do with what Jesus actually said or did. It' s like the experience I often have in researching medical information: when I actually read the original research on a subject, it is often quite different than the interpretations or conclusions that have been developed and accepted through the years. In the case of both medical science and the teachings of Jesus, it pays to go back to the original sources!

At this point, I have deliberately decided not to quote specific passages from the Gospel accounts to back up or illustrate my impressions; I feel that any selection might bias your views. You need to do what I did—read it all as quickly as possible to gain an overall impression rather than get hung up on specific passages that may or may not reflect a more generalized view. As a way of quickly organizing my thoughts and impressions, I present them in several categories.

THE JEWISHNESS OF JESUS

As so many modern scholars have observed, Jesus was clearly

grounded in his Jewish heritage and beliefs. For example, he constantly referred to and quoted from the Hebrew Scriptures. But many Christians have so removed Jesus from his real-life context that they scarcely acknowledge how deeply Jewish he was. I am reminded of a theologian who was trying to convince a Christian audience that Jesus was really Jewish; finally a member of the congregation said that maybe Jesus was Jewish but his mother—the blessed Virgin—certainly was not!

If I may be very simplistic and even trite, I would compare Jesus' feelings about his Jewish heritage to that of many modern Christians for the official teachings of their church—a true love-hate relationship. Maybe a more elegant way to put it is to say that in receiving his Jewish tradition he often transcended it without a wholesale repudiation. There is no question that Jesus was deeply in touch with the teachings and practices of the various expressions of the Judaism of his day. There is also no question that he was often deeply critical of some of the practices and emphases of his inherited religion. This is not the place to detail those opposing attitudes—read them for yourself. It is simply to point out how deeply religious he was at a human level. Whatever else he was, Jesus was also a practicing Jew, someone who believed in the God of Abraham and in the covenant between that God and the Jewish people.

THE HUMANNESS OF JESUS

Jesus was also very much in touch with other human beings at a real-life level. Overall, the Gospels do not portray a heavenly deity floating above the affairs of everyday life. According to their portraits Jesus was no celestial god in disguise. His obvious human feelings ranged from genuine sorrow and compassion to real anger. Indeed so intensely human was Jesus in the context of his time, especially in his healing encounters with "demon-possessed" people, that some of his contemporaries thought he was himself mentally disturbed! Clearly the Gospels are full of hints (and in the Gospel of John many outright claims) that Jesus was also divine. But for those who think the Gospels simply present Jesus as a sanitized deity, the full-blooded human being portrayed by the Gospel writers may come as a shock.

THE SURPRISING TEACHINGS OF JESUS

The teachings of Jesus are far more disturbing and surprising than are portrayed by the usually dry and stilted language of official church teaching and doctrine. I will mention just a few themes and impressions that especially grabbed my attention in reading all of the Gospels straight through.

Jesus speaks often about the coming kingdom of God in terms of judgment on the human conditions and religious practices of his time—how many would be left out and what kinds of people, often surprisingly, would be included. While there is a universal quality about his compassion for the poor and the outcast, there is often a stern and even frightening quality about his predictions of what the judgment of God will be like. Another example: Jesus' comments about "family values" are downright startling. There is no sweet portrait of a popular view of the typical American family—mom and dad and two kids living comfortably in the suburbs—found in the Gospels. Rather, Jesus sometimes admonishes his followers to leave their families and follow him. He also describes how his teachings and his call to the kingdom of God (the most recurrent theme in his teachings) will sometimes split families apart as some respond to his call and others do not.

Jesus' teachings about other social issues are also surprising, at least given the emphasis in so much current church discussions. For example, he says absolutely nothing about abortion or homosexuality but quite a bit—and negatively—about divorce. I personally find that quite startling when I consider how many modern Christians have accepted divorce but condemn abortion and homosexuality. Jesus also spends a lot of time suggesting how foolish and even evil it can be to pursue material possessions. Actually, most branches of modern Christianity acknowledge this theme (second only to the kingdom of God in amount of space devoted in the Gospels) even while they often accumulate large amounts of property. But it is still startling to read how often and sharply Jesus critiques the accumulation of wealth in his teaching and parables. Also, as a natural outgrowth of his own teaching, Jesus clearly shows more sympathy to the outcast and sinful than he does to the righteous and formally religious. Indeed, the Gospels are full of incidents and statements demonstrating Jesus' deep devotion to those in trouble; he seeks them out and often makes a point of going into their homes to eat with them—a very significant act of inclusion in Jewish culture.

Obviously I have not even begun to do justice to the full riches of the life and teachings of Jesus. I will come to those in more detail in the next section. But I do believe that these impressions are reasonable reactions to a complete first-time reading of the Gospels. I would certainly urge any of you who are intrigued by my first impressions to read the Gospels for yourself. And I am reminded of M. Scott Peck's reaction to his first reading of the Gospels after age forty and after the great success of his first book, *The Road Less Traveled*. He records his reaction in his follow-up book, *Further Along the Road Less Traveled*:

> I was absolutely thunderstruck by the extraordinary reality of the man I found in the Gospels. . . . I discovered a man so incredibly real that no one could have made Him up. It occurred to me then that if the Gospel writers had been into PR and embellishment, as I had assumed, they would have created the kind of Jesus three quarters of Christians still seem to be trying to create . . . portrayed with a sweet, unending smile on His face, patting little children on the head, just strolling the earth with this unflappable, unshakable equanimity. . . . But the Jesus of the Gospels—who some suggest is the best-kept secret of Christianity—did not have much "peace of mind," as we ordinarily think of peace of mind in the world's terms, and insofar as we can be His followers, perhaps we won't either. . . . It is as if most Christians haven't read the Gospels, and most Christian clergy are not even able to preach the real truth of the Gospels, because if they did, their congregations would flee out the door.[1]

Those last words I have quoted from Peck are obviously very provocative—basically accusing typical Christian church teaching and preaching of avoiding the "real truth" of the Gospel accounts of the life and teaching of Jesus. What is that "real truth," and why is it so often avoided?

A CLOSER LOOK AT JESUS

Before I go on to discuss some of the controversial or confusing events in the life of Jesus as reported in the Gospels and attempt to describe his meaning for me today, I would like to offer a further glance into his life and teaching, especially for those who have little or no familiarity with the New Testament Gospel accounts. I hinted at some of them in the previous section describing my first impressions, but now I would like to present selected passages by first quoting them directly and then offering my own brief and personal reactions as to their significance and meaning. (I will use a version of the New Testament translated from early texts by the United Bible Societies known as *The Bible in Today's English Version*.) I have forced myself to pick a top-twelve list (six events and six parables, two of which appear in the next section of this book). In this section I have left out what is undoubtedly the most provocative of Jesus' teachings—the astonishing Sermon on the Mount, which we will explore in section three. Obviously this arbitrary selection process is highly personal; others might choose differently. But these are the passages that have especially inspired or disturbed me, and I hope they will give you an appetite for more reading of the Gospels on your own.

He chose mercy over purity. I begin with six episodes in the life of Jesus that give some sense of the radical way he challenged the religious and social assumptions of his day. Central to those assumptions were the concepts of holiness and purity. For some segments of Judaism at the time of Jesus, those two concerns became so intertwined as to become almost synonymous. Thus for many religious Jews the way to stay holy was to stay pure. (Maybe that's how the admonition "cleanliness is next to godliness" got started.) One faction in Judaism that championed this viewpoint was the Pharisees, whose genuine piety sometimes became obsessively focused on ritual purity practices involving food preparation, personal hygiene and avoiding those regarded as unclean or sinful. Modern scholarship suggests that the Pharisees have gotten a bad rap by being identified so totally in popular perception with rigid legalism. But Jesus clearly saw such emphasis as contrary to the true heart of God, which was full of mercy and love for all humankind, even and especially so-called sinners. I have selected several episodes in which Jesus boldly challenged the focus on *purity* to the exclusion of *mercy*, beginning with the healing of a leper, an incident recorded in all three Synoptic Gospels.

BREAKING THE RULES TO HEAL

Once Jesus was in a town where there was a man who was suffering from a dreaded skin disease. When he saw Jesus, he threw himself down and begged him, "Sir, if you want to, you can make me clean!"

Jesus reached out and touched him. "I do want to," he answered. "Be clean!" At once the disease left the man. Jesus ordered him, "Don't tell anyone, but go straight to the priest and let him examine you; then to prove to everyone that you are cured, offer the sacrifice as Moses ordered."

But the news about Jesus spread all the more widely and crowds of people came to hear him and be healed from their diseases. But he would go away to lonely places, where he prayed. (Luke 5:12-16)

I begin with an instance of healing for several reasons. First, it goes right to the heart of Jesus' life and teachings in illustrating how he responded to human need as he encountered it. He quite literally reached out and touched people, even when that meant clearly violating the purity laws prohibiting physical contact with those afflicted with leprosy (a label that covered many different skin diseases). There is no more dramatic way Jesus could have demonstrated his focus on mercy versus purity.

However, at this early point in his ministry Jesus also tried to stay within the practices of Judaism by asking the man to follow temple protocol in having the priest certify him as being clean. As we will see though, Jesus would eventually lose his patience with the rigidity of some of the purity practices.

Second, this healing episode illustrates something else important to realize about Jesus—namely, he was not a frantic faith healer of the kind so often seen in modern times. Rather he went about his life in quiet fashion, healing when he could but often withdrawing from the crowds—a pattern that indicated a trust in God's ultimate mercy that did not require him to do it all himself.

WORDS FOR THE SELF-RIGHTEOUS

When Jesus finished speaking, a Pharisee invited him to eat with him; so he went in and sat down to eat. The Pharisee was surprised when he noticed that Jesus had not washed before eating. So the Lord said to him, "Now then, you Pharisees clean the outside of your cup and plate, but inside you are full of violence and evil. Fools! Did not God, who made the outside, also make the inside? But give what is in your cups and plates to the poor, and everything will be ritually clean for you.

"How terrible for you Pharisees! You give to God one tenth of the seasoning herbs, such as mint and rue and all the other

herbs, but you neglect justice and love for God. These you should practice, without neglecting the others. How terrible for you Pharisees! You love the reserved seats in the synagogues and to be greeted with respect in the marketplaces. How terrible for you! You are like unmarked graves which people walk on without knowing it." (Luke 11:37-44)

Jesus was constantly contrasting outer appearance with inner reality—a difference all of us understand when we examine our own lives. He was especially focused on the hypocrisy of religious practice. None of us likes to be confronted with our own hypocrisy. But Jesus did it constantly, with a bluntness that could sear the soul. Eventually, he paid a huge price for his candor, but he never seemed to lack the courage to do and say what he believed was right. It is an example rarely emulated.

A PROSTITUTE'S LAVISH DEVOTION

A Pharisee invited Jesus to have dinner with him, and Jesus went to his house and sat down to eat. In that town was a woman who lived a sinful life. She heard that Jesus was eating in the Pharisee's house, so she brought an alabaster jar full of perfume and stood behind Jesus, by his feet, crying and wetting his feet with her tears. Then she dried his feet with her hair, kissed them, and poured the perfume on them. When the Pharisee saw this, he said to himself. "If this man really were a prophet, he would know who this woman is who is touching him; he would know what kind of sinful life she lives!"

Jesus spoke up and said to him, "Simon, I have something to tell you."

"Yes, Teacher," he said, "tell me."

"There were two men who owed money to a moneylender," Jesus began. "One owed him five hundred silver coins, and the other one fifty. Neither of them could pay him back, so he canceled the debts of both. Which one, then, will love him more?"

"I suppose," answered Simon, "that it would be the one who was forgiven more."

"You are right," said Jesus. Then he turned to the woman and said to Simon, "Do you see this woman? I came into your home, and you gave me no water for my feet, but she has washed my feet with her tears and dried them with her hair. You did not welcome me with a kiss, but she has not stopped kissing my feet since I came. You provided no olive oil for my head, but she has covered my feet with perfume. I tell you, then, the great love she has shown proves that her many sins have been forgiven. But whoever has been forgiven little shows only a little love." (Luke 7:36-47)

Some Pharisees apparently made it their business not only to know the law but also to find out who was being "good" and who was being "bad." When a woman showed up to perform a loving act with a costly gift, they knew they had caught someone really bad. But unlike the Pharisees, Jesus didn't focus on her past behavior. Rather, he saw her future possibilities and loved her regardless of her past.

Is there really anything more wonderful than being truly forgiven and truly loved? Wouldn't you pour some perfume and cry your heart out for that gift of unconditional love in a world that shamed and rejected you?

JESUS AND THE CONDEMNED WOMAN

Early the next morning he went back to the Temple. All the people gathered around him, and he sat down and began to teach them. The teachers of the Law and the Pharisees brought in a woman who had been caught committing adultery, and they made her stand before them all. "Teacher," they said to Jesus, "this woman was caught in the very act of committing adultery. In our Law Moses commanded that such a woman must be stoned to death. Now, what do you say?" They said this to trap Jesus so that they could accuse him. But he bent over and wrote on the ground with his finger. As they stood there asking him questions, he straightened up and said to them, "Whichever one of you has committed no sin may throw the first stone at her." Then he bent over again and wrote on the ground. When they heard this, they all left, one by one, the older ones first. Jesus was left alone, with the woman still standing there. He straightened up and said to her, "Where are they? Is there no one left to condemn you?"

"No one, sir," she answered.

"Well, then," Jesus said, "I do not condemn you either. Go, but do not sin again." (John 8:2-11)

When Jesus' opponents brought to him a woman caught in adultery, this time they had actually captured someone in the very act—

according to Jewish law, punishable by death. (Typically, according to then-current standards, they didn't seem concerned about the man, who presumably was also part of the act.) And since they probably assumed Jesus would not condone stoning the woman, they thought they really had him this time; he would have to either deny their ancient law in public or endorse stoning the woman. But he dramatically reminded them that none of us is free of sin. And they slunk off, one by one, the older ones first because they knew right away they had been trapped in their own hypocrisy.

He warned the wealthy. I have chosen these last two episodes because they concern a theme that is second in Jesus' teaching only to the broad theme of the kingdom of God: the foolishness and futility of acquiring wealth for its own sake.

JESUS AND THE RICH YOUNG RULER

As Jesus was starting on his way again, a man ran up, knelt before him, and asked him, "Good Teacher, what must I do to receive eternal life?"

"Why do you call me good?" Jesus asked him. "No one is good except God alone. You know the commandments: 'Do not commit murder; do not commit adultery; do not steal; do not accuse anyone falsely; do not cheat; respect your father and your mother.'"

"Teacher," the man said, "ever since I was young I have obeyed all these commandments."

Jesus looked straight at him with love and said, "You need only one thing. Go and sell all you have and give the money to the

poor, and you will have riches in heaven; then come and follow
me." When the man heard this, gloom spread over his face, and
he went away sad, because he was very rich. (Mark 10:17-22)

[This incident is also recorded in Matthew and Luke, where
we learn that this rich man was also "young" and a "ruler."
Clearly he had also tried to live an exemplary life.]

Jesus had a startling way of zeroing in on the sore spot, the hidden
problem that was keeping a person from truly seeking God. Obviously, his prescription to sell everything and give the proceeds to the
poor is not appropriate for everyone. But maybe it is exactly the right
remedy for the person who has everything but feels as if he or she has
nothing worthwhile. And it is worth noting that Jesus apparently said
this not with anger or rejection but with love, not as a suggestion of
judgment but of redemption.

A SUDDEN CHANGE OF HEART

Jesus went on into Jericho and was passing through. There was
a chief tax collector there named Zacchaeus, who was rich. He
was trying to see who Jesus was, but he was a little man and
could not see Jesus because of the crowd. So he ran ahead of the
crowd and climbed a sycamore tree to see Jesus, who was going
to pass that way. When Jesus came to that place, he looked up
and said to Zacchaeus, "Hurry down, Zacchaeus, because I
must stay in your house today."

Zacchaeus hurried down and welcomed him with great joy.
All the people who saw it started grumbling, "This man has

> gone as a guest to the home of a sinner!"
>
> *Zacchaeus stood up and said to the Lord, "Listen, sir! I will give half my belongings to the poor, and if I have cheated anyone, I will pay him back four times as much."*
>
> *Jesus said to him, "Salvation has come to this house today, for this man, also, is a descendant of Abraham. The Son of Man came to seek and to save the lost."* (Luke 19:1-10)

To fully appreciate the irony of this encounter, it is important to know that as a chief tax collector, Zacchaeus could easily extort more than the fair tax from anyone he wanted, so he was hated as a "sinner." And once again Jesus quickly finds the sore spot, only this time he doesn't even have to say a word. Under the profound influence of the presence of Jesus, Zacchaeus does the right thing—he gives away half his fortune and restores fourfold to anyone he has cheated. And here is the truly remarkable result: by just doing the right thing with his money, he is awarded "salvation" and he becomes a "descendant of Abraham," welcomed into the fold! No statement of intellectual belief, no recitation of the commandments, just doing the "right thing." Is there a lesson for all of us here?

STORIES JESUS TOLD

Jesus taught by example, but he also taught by story. In the Bible the word *parable* covers a wide range of literary forms (including proverb, metaphor and allegory) that all have in common using illustrative material, often from the everyday life of the hearers. It is important to remember that in using parables, Jesus is trying to make a major point by using dramatic examples or details that are usually not to be taken literally. I begin with two parables that continue the theme of the dangers of money and possessions.

A FOOL AND HIS MONEY

There was once a rich man who had land which bore good crops. He began to think to himself, "I don't have a place to keep all my crops. What can I do? This is what I will do," he told himself; "I will tear down my barns and build bigger ones, where I will store the grain and all my other goods. Then I will say to myself, Lucky man! You have all the good things you need for many years. Take life easy, eat, drink, and enjoy yourself!" But God said to him, "You fool! This very night you will have to give up your life; then who will get all these things you have kept for yourself?"

And Jesus concluded, "This is how it is with those who pile up riches for themselves but are not rich in God's sight." (Luke 12:16-21)

Every time I read or hear this passage I get a chill up my spine. I can't imagine a worse label than "fool." (Call me anything, but don't call me a fool.) It is so obvious why this man is being foolish—pinning his ultimate hopes on his possessions—but he can' t stop himself and neither, most of the time, can we. Initially he may have been wise to invest in bigger barns for his crops, as any good farmer would. But somewhere along the way he gets caught up in the acquisition game and begins to worship "all [his] other goods" and believe that he has "all the good things [he needs] for many years."

Then the doctor says you have inoperable cancer, and suddenly you remember you can't take it with you. (Have you ever seen a hearse on the way to the cemetery with a U-Haul behind it?) What good are all those piled-up riches? Maybe they're helpful to your kids and charities, but certainly not to you when your number is called. So, warns Jesus, we better figure out what it means to be "rich in God's sight" before it is too late.

TOO LITTLE, TOO LATE

There was once a rich man who dressed in the most expensive clothes and lived in great luxury every day. There was also a poor man named Lazarus, covered with sores, who used to be brought to the rich man's door, hoping to eat the bits of food that fell from the rich man's table. Even the dogs would come and lick his sores. The poor man died and was carried by the angels to sit beside Abraham at the feast in heaven. The rich man died and was buried, and in Hades, where he was in great pain, he looked up and saw Abraham, far away, with Lazarus at this side. So he called out, "Father Abraham! Take pity on me, and send Lazarus to dip his finger in some water and cool off my tongue, because I am in great pain in this fire." But Abraham said, "Remember, my son, that in your lifetime you were given all the good things, while Lazarus got all the bad things. But now he is enjoying himself here, while you are in pain. Besides all that, there is a deep pit lying between us, so that those who want to cross over from here to you cannot do so, nor can anyone cross over to us from where you are." The rich man said, "Then I beg you, father Abraham, send Lazarus to my father's house, where I have five brothers. Let him go and warn them so that they, at least, will not come to this place of pain." Abraham said, "Your brothers have Moses and the prophets to warn them; your brothers should listen to what they say." The rich man answered, "That is not enough, father Abraham! But if someone were to rise from death and go to them, then they would turn from their sins." But Abraham said, "If they will not listen to Moses and the prophets, they will not be convinced even if someone were to rise from death." (Luke 16:19-31)

A little more complicated, this parable, but still crystal clear in its meaning. In very graphic terms Jesus describes the gulf that develops between God and those who allow their wealth to blind them to the needs of the poor right in front of their very eyes. And Jesus indicates we know what is right, what we ought to do. But would we be convinced of our wicked ways, like Scrooge, if someone came from "the other side" to warn us? Or would we, in real life versus a Dickens novel, doubt the messenger's authenticity and, once again, ignore the message?

THE GOOD SAMARITAN

There was once a man who was going down from Jerusalem to Jericho when robbers attacked him, stripped him, and beat him up, leaving him half dead. It so happened that a priest was going down that road; but when he saw the man, he walked on by on the other side. In the same way a Levite also came there, went over and looked at the man, and then walked on by on the other side. But a Samaritan who was traveling that way came upon the man, and when he saw him, his heart was filled with pity. He went over to him, poured oil and wine on his wounds and bandaged them; then he took him to an inn, where he took care of him. The next day he took out two silver coins and gave them to the innkeeper. "Take care of him," he told the innkeeper, "and when I come back this way, I will pay you whatever else you spend on him."

And Jesus concluded, "In your opinion, which one of these three acted like a neighbor toward the man attacked by the robbers?"

The teacher of the Law answered, "The one who was kind to him."

Jesus replied, "You go, then, and do the same." (Luke 10:30-37)

The parable of the Good Samaritan is one we can all relate to—whether or not we are rich—and therefore it is one that both encourages and condemns us all. This parable is told in response to a teacher of the law who asks Jesus how to inherit eternal life. Jesus answers by quoting the great commandment from Hebrew Scripture, "Love the Lord your God with all your heart and with all your soul and with all your strength and with all your mind and love your neighbor as yourself." The teacher of the law then asks, "Who is my neighbor?" Jesus gives him a surprising answer in this story, which features an ethnic twist.

To fully appreciate the irony and impact of this exchange, it is necessary to understand that most Jews of that time despised Samaritans, who were half-Jews, as it were, in their religious practice. They honored the Torah but not the Prophets, and they worshiped on Mount Gerizim to the north but not in the Jerusalem temple. So when the lawyer tried to trap Jesus with a legalese question, Jesus directed his response to the lawyer's own prejudice and arrogance by making a hated Samaritan the hero of his parable. Jesus cleverly turned the question on its head by saying that anyone in need is automatically our neighbor, and any of us can be a good Samaritan by simply, but not always easily, being kind and compassionate.

THE PRODIGAL SON

There was once a man who had two sons. The younger one said to him, "Father, give me my share of the property now." So the man divided his property between his two sons. After a few days the younger son sold his part of the property and left home with the money. He went to a country far away, where he wasted his money in reckless living. He spent everything he had. Then a severe famine spread over that country, and he was left without a thing. So he went to work for one of the citizens of that country, who sent him out to his farm to take care of the pigs. He wished he could fill himself with the bean pods the pigs ate, but no one gave him anything to eat. At last he came to his senses and said, "All my father's hired workers have more than they can eat, and here I am about to starve! I will get up and go to my father and say, 'Father, I have sinned against God and against you. I am no longer fit to be called your son; treat me as one of your hired workers.'" So he got up and started back to his father.

He was still a long way from home when his father saw him; his heart was filled with pity, and he ran, threw his arms around his son, and kissed him. "Father," the son said, "I have sinned against

God and against you, I am no longer fit to be called your son." But the father called to his servants. "Hurry!" he said. "Bring the best robe and put it on him. Put a ring on his finger and shoes on his feet. Then go and get the prize calf and kill it, and let us celebrate with a feast. For this son of mine was dead, but now he is alive; he was lost, but now he has been found." And so the feasting began.

In the meantime, the older son was out in the field. On his way back, when he came close to the house, he heard the music and dancing. So he called one of the servants and asked him, "What's going on?" "Your brother has come back home," the servant answered, "and your father has killed the prize calf, because he got him back safe and sound." The older brother was so angry that he would not go into the house, so his father came out and begged him to come in. But he spoke back to his father, "Look, all these years I have worked for you like a slave, and I have never disobeyed your orders. What have you given me? Not even a goat for me to have a feast with my friends! But this son of yours wasted all your property on prostitutes, and when he comes back home, you the kill the prize calf for him!" "My son," the father answered, "You are always here with me, and everything I have is yours. But we had to celebrate and be happy, because your brother was dead, but now he is alive, he was lost, but now he has been found." (Luke 15:11-31)

The parable of the prodigal son is for me one of the most emotionally moving of all the parables of Jesus. This stunning description of the love of God for even the most rebellious grabs us in the heart because it is put in the context of a father's love for a wayward son—a dynamic any parent (and I think any human) can immediately understand. But what gives this parable its edge is the apparent imbalance or unfairness of that love, lavishly poured out for the undeserving son while apparently ignoring the elder son, who represents the "resentful righteous" who think God's love can be earned. Not only is Jesus saying that the love of God is gladly willing to forgive past behavior, but he is also apparently saying that it is no different than what is available to the faithfully good person. Anyone at anytime who turns to God is welcomed—no questions asked, no special rewards given for good behavior other than the wonderful daily assurance that "everything I have is yours." By human standards it doesn't seem fair. But Jesus is saying that the love of God is lavish enough to include everyone who truly desires it.

RESPONDING TO JESUS

In his book *The Bible Speaks to You*, the late Robert McAfee Brown observed, "The fatal error is to read the Bible as a spectator rather than as a participant, to make the faulty assumption that we can sit in a box seat watching the drama, when actually we are on the stage taking part in the drama."[2] Many of us have found that the Bible—and particularly Jesus himself—has a compelling effect, insisting on a response. However, responding to what Jesus says means that we must come to grips with the question of his identity.

Questions of what Jesus said about himself and the implications of those claims for Bible readers can be very complex. Again, I want to emphasize the importance of entering into these questions for ourselves. We can find God in our own questions; we don't have to settle for others' answers. Jesus himself indicated that if we really want to know who he is and what he was up to, we can find out for ourselves. In that spirit, let's explore some possible approaches to addressing the issues of who Jesus was—or is.

7

WHO WAS JESUS?

❧

Admiring Jesus for his ethical teachings is one thing; embracing him as "the Son of God" is quite another. So who was this Jesus portrayed in the New Testament—this one whose life as presented in the Gospels has ever since produced a wide range of reactions, from deep devotion to scathing scorn?

By pure coincidence I found myself writing this section on a Palm Sunday—the day the Christian church celebrates Jesus' triumphant entry into Jerusalem, riding on a donkey with the crowd shouting "Hosanna" while strewing palm tree branches before his path. But this day also begins the week in which, in the same city, Jesus is crucified and buried and then reported to have risen from his grave. This story has inspired worship of Jesus as "the only begotten Son of God" and provoked outrage that such claims blaspheme the only one and true God. Like the often confused followers of Jesus in the New Testament, each new generation of readers must ask, "Who was Jesus?"

Whatever else he was, Jesus was very human. Theoretically there should be absolutely nothing surprising or shocking about this statement. Even the Christian church has long officially taught that Jesus was both "fully human" and "fully divine." However, the unofficial attitude of many Christians has been that the really important aspect of Jesus was his divinity. In its creeds and worship, the church has tended to highlight belief in the divinity of Jesus as the "Son of God" versus his very human earthly life. But when you read the Gospels, you cannot escape for a minute the impression that in many different ways Jesus lived as a very real human being.

I believe the crux of this issue of Jesus' identity as human and/or divine rests in three aspects of the New Testament record of his life, which have often been controversial or confusing for modern readers: his reported miracles, the meaning of his crucifixion and the significance of his reported resurrection. For many people, Jesus' teachings, as sampled in previous chapters, are inspiring, but these events presented in support of his divinity are often "stumbling blocks" to any further consideration of his potential relevance to modern men and women.

THE MIRACLES

The four Gospels report about three dozen miracles performed by Jesus—often categorized into three groups: miraculous feedings (the only miracle recorded in all four Gospels is the feeding of the five thousand from a small basket of food), nature miracles (walking on water, stilling a storm), and healings and exorcisms (by far the largest group). Some are clearly more palatable to the skeptical mind than others; many people can accept "casting out demons" as an ancient (and very efficient) form of psychotherapy. But others are much harder to swallow for rational moderns, who often see the miracles as an attempt to portray Jesus as a kind of magician. Many people feel like doing what Thomas Jefferson actually did—he cut and pasted together a version of the New Testament that preserved Jesus' teachings but eliminated all the miracle stories. (That document is in the Smithsonian Institution in Washington, D.C.)

I personally was brought up on a steady diet of miracle stories from both the Old and New Testaments. And as a child they all seemed "natural" to me. In my childlike innocence I figured that any God who could create the heavens and the earth in seven days could certainly pull off a little miracle here and there. Of course, now that I "understand" that this universe actually exploded out of nothing and went from a pinhead to a massive broiling ball of gases in far less than a millisecond, how can I possibly believe in miracles anymore? (That's tongue-in-cheek, folks). Or should I say today that any God who could create the cosmos as we are now beginning to dimly understand it could certainly do such piddly things as calm a storm or heal people or even raise them from the dead?

I am reminded of Saint Augustine's famous statement that miracles are not contrary to nature, but only contrary to what we know about nature. But believing that modern science suggests that "anything seems possible" is different than proving that the miracles attributed to Jesus actually happened. The simple fact is that we can never prove, according to today's accepted standards of proof, whether or not any of these miracles actually happened. We have no audio or video recordings; we can't reproduce the exact conditions in which these miracles are reported to have occurred. So the larger question in the context of this book is this: Does it make a significant difference in your ultimate view of Jesus whether or not you can believe he performed miracles?

The answer to this question, of course, depends on what you mean by "significant difference." If belief in miracles is a precondition for giving the overall life and teachings of Jesus any kind of consideration, then such belief would be very significant. But the Gospels seem to indicate that Jesus himself did not insist on belief in miracles as a precondition for following him or for spiritual growth. In fact Jesus often downplayed his miracles and sometimes asked the beneficiaries of his healings not to tell anyone what happened, as if he knew the reporting of them would cause more trouble than they were worth in any spiritual sense.

I have never met a person who believes in God because he or she first believed in miracles, but I have met a lot of people who, because they believe in God, think miracles can happen. And for what it is worth, I will tell you that, paradoxically, the more I have come to believe in the possibility of miracles because of my growing understanding of the nature of the universe, the less important they have become to my belief in God or my understanding of Jesus.

THE CRUCIFIXION

One common objection to a popular understanding of traditional Christian doctrine about the crucifixion goes something like this: I can accept that Jesus was crucified because of the way he upset the religious and political leaders of his time, but I can't accept the idea that he had to be sacrificed according to some inevitable plan to appease God's demand for justice or payment for the sins of humankind. Other more logical objectors point out the incongruity of "God killing God," which would be one implication of the crucifixion according to an absolutely literal interpretation of church doctrine that teaches that Jesus is "true God of true God" and is of the same "substance" as God. In fact, taking all of the New Testament accounts of Jesus' death together, we are left with an apparent paradox—something that was so wrong (the killing of an innocent man) was also so good (the means of salvation for humankind).

The Gospel writers clearly considered the events of Holy Week to be of paramount importance; they devoted about a third of their accounts to the events surrounding Jesus' death. And it is quite obvious that by the time New Testament authors wrote down the accounts of that week, various theological interpretations had been woven into those accounts. But I will paraphrase what I just said about miracles: I have never met anyone who came to believe in the love and forgiveness of God because they first figured out the exact theological meaning of Jesus' crucifixion. But I have met many people who, because they believe in a loving and forgiving God, see in Jesus' death the supreme example of that love and forgiveness.

It is this theme of the forgiving power of love that M. Scott Peck references in his provocative book *People of the Lie:*

I cannot be any more specific about the methodology of love than to quote these words of an old priest who spent many years in the battle: "There are dozens of ways to deal with evil and several ways to conquer it. All of them are facets of the truth that the only ultimate way to conquer evil is to let it be smothered within a willing, living human being. When it is absorbed there like blood in a sponge or a spear into one's heart, it loses its power and goes no further." . . . The healing of evil— scientifically or otherwise—can be accomplished only by the love of individuals. A willing sacrifice is required. The individual healer must allow his or her own soul to become the battleground. He or she must sacrificially absorb the evil. . . . I do not know how this occurs. But I know that it does. . . . Whenever this happens there is a slight shift in the balance of power in the world.[1]

Christian doctrine, of course, claims that a major shift in the balance between good and evil occurred because of Jesus' willingness to "sacrificially absorb the evil." And given the enormous good that has since been done in the name of Jesus, there is good reason to support this claim. Unfortunately, much evil has also been done in the name of Jesus, especially by those who irrationally hold all Jews since the time of Jesus responsible for his death. (I would refer you to the brief but brilliant article on anti-Semitism in the *Oxford Companion to the Bible* by former Harvard Divinity School dean Krister Stendahl.) The clear fact emerging from the Gospel accounts of Jesus' death is that the final decision allowing Jesus to be crucified was made by the sitting Roman governor, Pontius Pilate. And I have little doubt that if Jesus showed up today teaching and preaching in the same way, the religious and political leaders of our time, both non-Jewish and Jewish, would figure out some way to quickly marginalize or discredit his disturbing teachings. We are too civilized to crucify him, but we would try to get him out of the way and out of our lives as soon as possible.

Indeed, part of the problem with formulaic and dogmatic thinking about the crucifixion is that it often lets us off the hook personally. In a provocative book titled *Growing Up Fundamentalist*, Stephan Ulstein quotes from one of his interviews a college administrator who felt he had been misled by his dogmatic upbringing:

For instance, the fundamentalist view of the passion is that Christ had to die for our sins to accomplish our salvation. So the whole passion narrative just leads up to that one point like a train running down a preordained track. I wondered: if that was true, then why didn't he just come down to earth and get it over with? Why all the drama if it could have ended only one way and if he knew how it would end anyway?

If you really read the passion narratives, they are about Christ antagonizing the powers that be. He ticked people off and challenged their authority. It's a much more human and social dynamic than just marching to a predetermined conclusion. All that interaction between Jesus and the various people wasn't just to make a theological point. . . .

But you miss all that when you reduce the passion to a theological formula that says there *had* to be a price. When you reduce it to an inevitable chain of events, you get to blame the crucifixion on "them." That's not the point. . . . It takes us out of the picture, reduces us to observers when we are really players.[2]

I couldn't agree more! In fact, the more I read convoluted human explanations about "the meaning of the crucifixion," the more it seems to me that unnecessary conclusions are likely to result when we insist on rational or dogmatic formulas for something that is ultimately inexplicable in human words—the power of God's love to forgive and "wipe out" even the most horrible evil. I personally find the death of Jesus on the cross to be a monumental example of what happens when good confronts evil, when love encounters hatred. And I find Jesus' willingness to forgive even those who crucified him an indelible portrait of the power of such forgiveness in human affairs; it is an example that has inspired such nonviolent revolutionary leaders as Mahatma Gandhi and Martin Luther King Jr. to use the power of love instead of the power of arms. I am even willing to see in Jesus' death a divinely ordained message about the intent of God to show love and forgiveness for us in any way necessary.

I also increasingly see the crucifixion of Jesus as something that happened because of me—and people like me—rather than something that had to happen for God. I have come to recognize that I need to be forgiven for the way I have lived—and that in some mysterious way, the death of Jesus offers me forgiveness. I must also confess that the story of Jesus' crucifixion for me is more than just the story of how the forgiveness of God is so supremely demonstrated in the death of this one who was "without sin." Even though I cannot put its meaning easily into human words and theological formulas, I have always found the story of Jesus' crucifixion to offer the hope that evil can sometimes be overcome in this life—and that it has been overcome in some ultimate sense that we will fully understand only in the life to come. (See pp. 175-80 for a discussion of suffering and life after death.)

The remarkable expansion of the Christian religion throughout Africa and South America today is occurring largely because of the hope that the story of Jesus brings to people living in devastating poverty and disease. I know this sounds mystical and mysterious, but I also know that the telling of the story of Jesus' crucifixion year after year during Holy Week has indeed been the "power of salvation" for those who respond to the story with belief that the God of creation has entered human history on our behalf—and overcome evil on our behalf. And that belief is of course tied to the conviction that Jesus was raised from the dead as the ultimate sign of God's message that evil and even death itself will ultimately be overcome. So it is to this pivotal event that I now turn my attention.

THE RESURRECTION

In his intriguing novel *A Prayer for Owen Meany* (which was made into the movie *Simon Birch*), John Irving has the narrator say:

> I find that Holy Week is draining; no matter how many times I have lived through his crucifixion, my anxiety about his resurrection is undiminished—I am terrified that, this year, it won't happen; that, that year, it didn't. Anyone can be sentimental about the Nativity; any fool can feel like a Christian at Christmas. But Easter is the main event; if you don't believe in the resurrection, you're not a believer.[3]

The apostle Paul puts it just as bluntly in his letter to the early church at Corinth: "If Christ has not been raised, then our preaching is in vain, and your faith is in vain" (1 Corinthians 15:14). So, are the apostle Paul and John Irving's character correct: if you don't believe in the resurrection, you are not a true believer and certainly not a Christian in any traditional sense? Before answering that question with my own point of view, let's look at the New Testament accounts of the resurrection.

First, contrary to a popular misunderstanding, the New Testament does not describe Jesus' resurrection as a first century resuscitation—that is, the restoration of his dead body from a "clinical death" to its previous physical state. If Jesus had simply shown up just as he was before death, the logical assumption might have been that he never really died, and it is unlikely that there would have been all the confusion and doubt, so honestly recorded in the Gospel accounts, about his new appearance. Rather, taking all the Gospel accounts of the resurrection together, it is clear that the "new" Jesus they report seeing and even touching is significantly different from the old one. Exactly what kind of "new body" is not clear, but it definitely is not just a resuscitated traditional body. (The apostle Paul reflects this just a few decades after these events in his letter to the Corinthians when he tries to explain the difference between a "physical body" and a "spiritual body" and says, "The body that is sown is perishable, it is raised imperishable; it is sown in dishonor, it is raised in glory; it is sown in weakness, it is raised in power; it is sown a natural body, it is raised a spiritual body" [1 Corinthians 15:42-44 NIV].) Ultimately, it probably is just as hard to believe in a resurrected spiritual body as in a resuscitated physical body, but given the incomprehensible world of modern physics in which WIMPS may be constantly passing through our bodies (see p. 35), the possibility of new physical realities contrary to our usual experience seems entirely possible to me.

Second, there appears to be no doubt about the empty tomb, but that really doesn't mean much in and of itself. An empty tomb could mean anything from a true resurrection to a plot in which Jesus' body was stolen. But if the empty tomb occurred because Jesus' followers had stolen his body, you would think that the Roman and Jewish authorities would have spared no effort to find the body in order to quell the troublesome rumors about Jesus' resurrection, rumors that would contribute to subsequent trouble for the Roman government and great embarrassment for the religious leaders who so wanted to discredit Jesus. Indeed, the account in Matthew's Gospel describes how the Roman soldiers charged with guarding the tomb went to the chief priests to report what had happened and were told, "You are to say that his disciples came during the night and stole his body while you were asleep. And if the Governor should hear of this, we will convince him that you are innocent, and you will have nothing to worry about" (Matthew 28:13-14). It would seem unlikely that all the guards could sleep through the commotion caused by rolling away the huge guarding stone and then carrying off of the body, but that's the story they came up with—even though no body was ever reported to be found!

There is one other telling point in the Gospel accounts of the resurrection—the first witnesses to Jesus' postresurrection appearances were reported to have been women. Given that the testimony of women was generally regarded with such low esteem in the ancient Semitic world, if the Gospel writers were making it all up they surely would have made the first witnesses male instead of female.

Third and most significantly, it seems very unlikely that anything other than a real resurrection would have led, within weeks after the crucifixion, to the bold group of believers who fueled the explosive growth of the Jesus Movement during the next twenty-five years under the frequent threat of persecution. Indeed, almost all scholars agree that it was their belief in the resurrection that primarily fueled the incredible growth of the Jesus Movement. In fact, there were at least a dozen other movements that arose within a hundred years on either side of the time of Jesus, led by charismatic Jews who announced that they could lead their people out of bondage to Rome. But in every case their death also led to the death of their movement. So why did Jesus' death not result in the same fate? From a purely historical point of view it seems logical to conclude that a belief that Jesus had truly been raised from the dead was the main reason that the Jesus Movement succeeded where all others failed. In other words, whether or not you can believe in the resurrection now, two thousand years removed from the time of Jesus, there is no doubt that his early followers fervently believed in the fact that somehow God had raised Jesus from the dead. And I personally believe that the otherwise unexplainable success of the early Jesus Movement verifies the reality of the resurrection; in other words, I believe it really happened.

Now back to my question: Do you have to believe in the resurrection to be an orthodox Christian? I think the answer is clearly yes. But do you first have to believe in the resurrection to become a follower of Jesus? The answer would seem to be no, simply because the first followers of Jesus described in the New Testament knew nothing about his eventual resurrection when they decided to become his followers. I do believe that if you choose to follow Jesus, you will eventually believe in his resurrection. But you need not start with such an intellectual mind-bender. Indeed, the earliest members of the Jesus Movement knew nothing about creeds or orthodox belief in our sense of these words. They were simply and yet profoundly attracted to the person and teaching of this itinerant peasant named Joshua (his probable Hebrew name). And so it is time to finally address the questions raised at the beginning of this chapter: who was this Jesus and what should modern, sophisticated folk like us make of the claims that he was and is God?

FROM THE GOSPELS OF THE JESUS MOVEMENT TO THE CREEDS OF THE CHURCH

The overall portrait of Jesus in the Synoptic (the first three) Gospels sometimes seems quite different than the one in the Gospel of John, widely regarded as the last to be written. In Matthew, Mark and

Luke, Jesus is often more mysterious about his identify, at times even self-effacing. Recall the story of the rich young ruler from the Gospel of Mark: "As Jesus was starting on his way again, a man ran up, knelt before him, and asked him, 'Good Teacher, what must I do to receive eternal life?' 'Why do you call me good?' Jesus asked him. 'No one is good except God alone' " (Mark 10:17-18). These particular words of Jesus hardly sound like someone claiming to be God! But in the Gospel of John, Jesus is typically more bold in his claims, such as his statement, "The Father and I are One" (John 10:30).

Any honest and plain reading of those two statements back to back suggests differences in attitude on the part of Jesus—or at least different aspects of Jesus' understanding of his relationship to God. How could this be? Did different Gospel writers simply record a different emphasis from Jesus? Did Jesus himself develop a different understanding of who he was during his brief lifetime? Or did the followers of Jesus expand and refine their thinking about who he really was as they had more time to reflect on the meaning of his life? In fact, there is a fundamental difference in both style and content of the first three Gospels and the Gospel of John. For example, John's Gospel doesn't contain a single parable, unlike the Synoptics, which contain many; instead John has many long speeches from the mouth of Jesus. The Synoptics start with details about the birth or early ministry of the human Jesus. In staggering contrast the Gospel of John starts with an elegant theological statement about the cosmic origin of Jesus, words that are clearly a reflection of the opening words in Genesis:

> In the beginning was the Word, and the Word was with God, and the Word was God. He was with God in the beginning.

> Through him all things were made; without him nothing was made that
> has been made. In him was life, and that life was the light of men. The
> light shines in the darkness, but the darkness has not understood it. . . .
>
> The Word became flesh and made his dwelling among us. We have
> seen his glory, the glory of the One and Only, who came from the Father,
> full of grace and truth. (John 1:1-5, 14 NIV)

This piece of theological poetry uses the concept of *Logos* (Greek
for "Word") to describe Jesus as the "Wisdom" or "Word" of God that
is now being revealed "in the flesh," in the life of a real human being.
For Jesus' followers, it then became a rather logical jump to describe
Jesus as the "Son of God." It is hard to avoid the conclusion that at
least some of the growing emphasis on the divinity of Jesus occurred
in the context of the unfolding struggle of the early Jesus Movement
in the first century. The early followers of Jesus were also Jews who
worshiped God, but during the last half of the first century they increasingly began to differentiate themselves from developing rabbinical Judaism that did not accept Jesus as the promised Messiah.
Thomas Cahill graphically describes the subsequent impact of these
developments on Jewish-Christian relations through the centuries:

> But if it may be said that the rabbinical Jews won this first century tug-
> of-war and continued to hold the upper hand for the next two centuries,
> the tide will turn in the early fourth century with the emperor Constan-
> tine's induction as a Christian . . . after which Christians will spend the
> next sixteen and a half centuries rounding up Jews, hunting them down,
> depriving them of civil rights, torturing, massacring, and ridiculing to
> their heart's content. This centuries-long pogrom is the lasting shame of
> Christianity. . . . As has so often been the case in religious history, the very
> thing that one is rejected for becomes the treasure one must never give

up—a treasure that is emphasized, exaggerated, and made into one's badge of honor. It is just such a psychological process that creates obsessive positions that can bear no compromise—and that finally makes dialogue (between Jews and Christians, as well as among varieties of Christians) impossible.[4]

This very brief summary combines what actually happened historically with a possible psychological or religious motivation—that is, making "a treasure" (Jesus) into an obsessive "badge of honor" (something that makes us think we are better than those who believe differently and in worse form gives us spiritual permission to persecute them). It is certainly true that from the moment Emperor Constantine declared Christianity to be an acceptable religion in the Roman Empire in the early fourth century, theological positions hardened (some would say ossified) and the hatred of the subsequent centuries against Jews started to heat up. According to Marvin Wilson, in his wonderfully detailed account of the Jewish roots of Christianity (see "Suggested Reading"), it was at this time that Jews lost many of their legal rights, including the right to dwell in Jerusalem.

In fact, in the early fourth century Constantine often interjected himself into church affairs. And in A.D. 325, in what turned out to be a watershed moment in religious history, Constantine ordered the bishops of his empire to meet in Nicea, a lakeside town southeast of Constantinople where he maintained a summer palace. He charged them to hammer out a creed that would eliminate the theological quarreling among themselves about the exact relationship of Jesus to God. They came up with language that, as subsequently modified at a later church council, reads in part as follows:

> We, then, following the holy Fathers, all with one consent, teach men to
> confess one and the same Son, our Lord Jesus Christ, the same perfect in
> God-head and also perfect in manhood; truly God and truly man, of a
> reasonable soul and body, consubstantial with the Father according to
> the Godhead, and consubstantial with us according to the manhood, in
> all things like unto us, without sin; begotten before all ages of the Father
> according to the Godhead. . . . Only-begotten, in two natures, incon-
> fusedly, unchangeably, indivisibly, inseparably, the distinction of natures
> being by no means taken away by the union, but rather the property of
> each nature being preserved, and concurring in one person and one sub-
> sistence, not parted or divided into two persons, but one and the same
> Son and Only-begotten, God the Word, the Lord Jesus Christ.[5]

It is enough to make me weep—this reduction of the vibrant Jesus portrayed in the Gospels to the stilted language of church leaders under pressure from the emperor to settle their theological differences. (No separation of church and state here!) It is almost as if they had turned the profoundly beautiful relationship between Jesus and God as recorded in the Gospels into a basic biology lesson! From this moment on, the course was set. Not only would the church increasingly define its beliefs and practice through highly intellectualized creedal statements, but the humble organization of the initial Jesus Movement would eventually become the imperial church sanctioned by imperial Rome. It would become a political and even military-like force that would often elevate itself to the heights of secular power and prestige but all too often at the spiritual expense of distorting the original message of Jesus.[6]

I believe that if Jesus were to return to earth today, he would be stunned and saddened to see that the church founded in his name has too often become a gathering of those more concerned to be politically influential or socially powerful than to be spiritually available to those in need. Indeed when I see parts of the church today on display with fine robes and crowns of jewels, and think about Jesus dying on the cross with his simple peasant clothes ripped and torn, my heart breaks over the way we humans have so often distorted or ignored the teachings of Jesus. Can we really believe that if Jesus came to earth today, he would be dressed in lavish robes and bejeweled crowns? And if he wouldn't, why should we?

This is just one of many reasons why I have come to prefer the phrase a "follower of Jesus" rather than the label "Christian." The latter word too often simply indicates blind support of the various aspects of the religion called Christianity. (The word *Christianity*, designating a formal religion, is not found in the New Testament and is first used by a Roman historian in the second century.) I personally like "follower of Jesus" for many reasons, including

- It drives me back to the Gospel accounts of the life and teachings of Jesus as my spiritual guide. It puts me in the good company of the first followers of Jesus who knew nothing of the later intellectual formulations that would transform the Jesus they had experienced in real life into the Christ of the creeds and the church.

- It does not force me into explaining what kind of Christian I am or am not—for example, a "Jerry Falwell" Christian or a "Bishop Spong" Christian, both of whom claim to be Christians but are as different as night and day in what they believe and teach.

- It does not require me to defend the terrible misdeeds of some past representatives of the Christian religion or to justify the cultural stridency of some modern Christians. It also frees me from playing the endless and divisive intellectual game of who is "right" and which theological positions (all of them too human in their verbal formulations) are "true." Indeed, sometimes the shouting match between so-called believers begins to sound like that of children in a theological sandbox screaming, "My God is better than your God!" The terrible religious hatred of recent times reminds us just how dangerous that theological sandbox fighting can become. If there is one thing I am now absolutely certain of, it is that no human minds or committees will ever capture the powerful reality we call God with human words or formulas or creeds. At best, and even then only a distant second best, they can be only an approximation of that reality.

Most important, calling myself a follower of Jesus urges me to pursue the kind of life portrayed and taught by Jesus in the Gospels. Indeed, the Gospel writer Luke, in his history of the early church as recorded in the book of Acts, often refers to the early followers of Jesus as those who followed the "Way of the Lord." I like the spiritual feel and sound of that phrase, implying a personal commitment of the heart to the "Way of Jesus" rather than a mental commitment to the intellectual formulations of church theologians.

I need to clarify that while I obviously have some quarrels with the intellectual formulations and actions of some parts of the church, I also recognize that this very same institution (and its members) has often been incredibly responsive to human needs, especially in the areas of education, health care and the alleviation of poverty. Care for the homeless, for widows and orphans, and for the suffering and dying has been championed by many Christian institutions through-out the world. And the church that at times in the past has shamefully been a defender of slavery and women's oppression has often worked for abolition and women's rights.

I should also acknowledge that I have been a lifelong member of various congregations within my own Protestant denomination. Indeed I can't imagine surviving spiritually without the nurture and love provided by these communities of faith as we have struggled to be followers of Jesus, of the "Way of the Lord."

So why do I even bother struggling to follow the "Way of the Lord"? The profound truth is that every day, each of us makes decisions about how we will live from moment to moment—how we will treat people and what we will spend our time and money pursuing. Most of the time we make those choices according to instinctive patterns developed over a long period of time. Whether we realize it or not, these routine daily choices are based on our philosophy of life, on the way we have chosen to follow. Indeed, all of us have a life philosophy even though we rarely discuss or articulate it as such. Usually, in fact, we live without much thought, guided by role models and ideals (parents, friends, celebrities, teachers, cultural fads, advertising, TV, movies, music) that subconsciously influence our moral and intellectual choices.

To put it very bluntly, even though I have been exposed to a wide range of philosophies, role models and cultural patterns, I have yet to find one that is more compelling and challenging than the life and teachings of this ancient Jew as presented in the Gospels. Indeed, I believe that Jesus of Nazareth reveals or portrays as fully as is possible within the confines of a human life the spirit of God, the mind of the Creator of the universe. In that sense I affirm the concept of the incarnation, which says that in Jesus we can begin to encounter and understand the otherwise ineffable and elusive reality called God.

One of my close friends, who is Jewish, responded to this idea by writing me:

> I had trouble following the logic that sustains your desire to continue as a follower of Jesus. You acknowledge that the information about Jesus is second or third hand, set down 70 or so years after his death. . . . In fact, I don't understand the logic you use for requiring ANY historical figure to buttress your faith. . . . Surely an individual can be a "good person" based on their belief in a higher being and his or her own intrinsic moral imperative.[7]

I definitely agree with the last part of his statement—that it is possible to be a "good person" without being a follower of Jesus. But I believe there are both practical and theological reasons to consider following the teachings of Jesus as presented in the Gospels. (And again I point out that the earliest references to Jesus in the New Testament—in the letters of the apostle Paul—were written down only about twenty years after his death, and that the oral tradition which led to the writing of the Gospels was a very reliable form of communication in ancient times.)

The practical reason, as I said, is the value of having role models and teachers in life. (It is not surprising that in the Gospels, Jesus is often addressed as "good teacher.") Some of us can live good lives without such guidance, but many of us will benefit from studying the historical Jesus whose life and teachings are presented in such understandable and dramatic fashion in the Gospel accounts.

However, it is time for me also to clearly state that I truly believe

Jesus is a critically important revelation of the same creator God I believe set this universe into motion and sustains it even now. Indeed I find his life and teachings to be uniquely valuable in trying to understand the intentions of that creator God as to how we should live.

THE MEANING OF SALVATION AND THE UNIQUENESS OF JESUS

Before I get to a specific discussion of the uniqueness of Jesus and whether Jesus is the Son of God, I should address one of the most divisive issues between some Christians and other religions: the claim that Jesus is the only way to salvation. Right up front I should tell you that the word *salvation* is very problematic both inside and outside of religious circles. For many Christians the explanation of the word often involves language about "believing in Jesus" or "accepting Jesus into my heart." To the outsider, this kind of talk sounds mystical at best, bizarre at worst.

It may help to begin by considering the word *saved* as it is widely used in everyday language—such as someone who is "saved" from a burning building or "saved" from a life of self-destruction. In this context the best synonym is probably *rescued*—the removal from a dangerous situation. Quite frankly, many who freely use the word *saved* in a religious context probably have little more understanding than this common meaning: they feel that their faith or their religious commitment has quite literally rescued them from a prior life of danger and degradation that was self-destructive. Typical of this kind of "conversion" is the alcoholic who credits "giving his heart to Jesus" as literally saving his life.

However, traditional church teaching invests the words *saved* and *salvation* with more theoretical and theological significance involving a "transaction" that changes a person's relationship with God—and, in some understandings, quite literally saves a person from eternal damnation and the fires of hell. It is beyond the scope of this book to present a thorough discussion of the many aspects of church teaching about salvation. But I would indicate that such teaching can range from an emphasis on *justice* (placating or appeasing a just God for our sins) to *mercy* (God showing love for us through the death of Jesus who somehow pays for our sins in that act of sacrifice).

These emphases on justice and mercy were part of the rationale for animal sacrifice so prominent in the early history of Israel and an important practice in temple worship even in Jesus' time. So while animal sacrifice seems irrational or even evil to most moderns, it is important to understand that it was a common part of Jewish religious life—and therefore naturally incorporated into language often found in the New Testament about the meaning of the death of Jesus. For example, in his letter to the church at Rome, the apostle Paul writes, "But God demonstrates his own love for us in this: While we were still sinners, Christ died for us. Since we have now been justified by his blood, how much more shall we be saved from God's wrath through him!" (Romans 5:8-9 NIV). In that brief passage the apostle Paul includes several concepts (the love of God for humanity, justification by blood, being saved from God's wrath) that were understandable to his first-century readers but are strangely foreign to most moderns not raised on the language of the Bible.

However, during the many centuries since, many branches of the Christian church have moved beyond such concepts of "justice" and "sacrifice" to understand "being saved" as a loving and personal relationship with God through Jesus that changes one's life for the better. In this sense "believing in Jesus" becomes an act of personal rescue and restoration—rescue from a life of sin and restoration to the life that God intends for all humans. This is the context in which the label often used by some Christians—"born again"—can best be understood. Those words come very specifically from an episode recorded in the third chapter of the Gospel of John:

> Now there was a man of the Pharisees named Nicodemus, a member of the Jewish ruling council. He came to Jesus at night and said, "Rabbi, we know you are a teacher who has come from God. For no one could perform the miraculous signs you are doing if God were not with him."
>
> In reply Jesus declared, "I tell you the truth, no one can see the kingdom of God unless he is born again."
>
> "How can a man be born when he is old?" Nicodemus asked. "Surely he cannot enter a second time into his mother's womb to be born!"
>
> Jesus answered, "I tell you the truth, no one can enter the kingdom of God unless he is born of water and the Spirit. Flesh gives birth to flesh, but the Spirit gives birth to spirit. You should not be surprised at my saying, 'You must be born again.'" (John 3:1-7 NIV)

One way to interpret this passage is to take it quite literally in the context of the person being addressed—Nicodemus. He is described as "a member of the Jewish ruling council," meaning that he was an elite Jewish man who undoubtedly took his heritage very seriously. So, as is so often the case in his encounters with fellow human beings, Jesus zeros in on Nicodemus's vulnerable point—in this case, his probable pride about his birthright. Therefore Jesus challenges him by saying that he cannot "see the kingdom of God" unless he is figuratively willing to give up what he prizes the most and be "born again" as a new person without pride regarding the privilege of his natural birth. Indeed, if you recall some of the New Testament passages quoted earlier about encounters between Jesus and those seeking his counsel, you will often see a common theme: Jesus sensing what is blocking them from seeking the kingdom of God. In the case of the rich young ruler it was his money—so Jesus asks him to give it to the poor. In the case of Zacchaeus it was also his riches resulting from his position of power—so Jesus inspires him to give half of his belongings to the poor and to repay anyone he has cheated fourfold. (And in that case Jesus explicitly says that "salvation" had come to Zacchaeus.) In the case of the prostitute, Jesus recognizes that she has become dependent on the money she gets from selling sex—so he praises her for being willing to pour out her perfume as a dramatic act of generous repentance. In all these cases Jesus is asking the person to be "born again" by giving up what is most precious and starting over in a new life dedicated to the kingdom of God.

In short, I believe this phrase—"born again"—should be understood metaphorically to describe a dramatic spiritual change in a person's life, so dramatic that it is reminiscent of our initial physical birth—a conversion from one kind of existence (in the womb) to another (in the outside world). Many people report their lives having been dramatically changed when they are confronted with the life and teachings of Jesus; their lives are radically reordered by believing in the power of Jesus' message to rescue them from their sinful ways and restore them to the life God intended.

However, these words have also become a catch phrase in some Christian circles for judgmental exclusivity, for differentiating a specific kind of religious experience (sudden and dramatic) from other "less valuable" forms of religious pilgrimage. Predictably, the meanings of the phrases "believing in Jesus" or "accepting Jesus as my Savior" are often very vague or ambiguous, even for those using them. If you ask them to describe what those words mean, they often can't do so with any precision. And in worse case scenarios these words are used cheaply or arrogantly without any commitment to personal change or ongoing spiritual growth. People can talk about "being saved" without any intention of changing the way they live. Conversely, people can experience profound change in their lives without any sophisticated theological understanding of "being saved."

Personally, I am increasingly uncomfortable with popular language about "being saved" or "being born again" precisely because these words are often used so imprecisely and so glibly. I do believe in the reality of sin and evil, and I do believe that we humans need to be changed in our hearts in order to truly change the way we live. But I don't believe that using verbal slogans is equivalent to being saved in the profound personal sense of being enabled to live a new life. Ultimately, I believe "being saved" is a lifelong process, a constant commitment of renewal. And I believe that what God requires of us in this lifelong process is best described by Jesus: when a lawyer asked him what is the great commandment in the law, Jesus replied by quoting from the Jewish Scripture he knew so well: "Love the Lord your God with all your heart and with all your soul and with all your mind. This is the first and greatest commandment. And the second is like it: Love your neighbor as yourself. All the Law and the Prophets hang on these two commandments" (Matthew 22:37-39 NIV).

What about the claims made by some Christians that only by "believing in Jesus" can we be loved and accepted by God? That claim usually comes directly from a passage in the Gospel of John. In chapter fourteen, Jesus is reported as saying, "I am the way, the truth and the life. No one comes to the Father except through me" (John 14:6 NIV). On the face of it this claim sounds incredibly arrogant and exclusive. How should we understand it?

At one level, I think there is good reason to take the passage at face value — namely, the idea that it is in the life and teaching of Jesus that we encounter the most in-depth understanding of God as Father. Many scholars acknowledge that the uniqueness of Jesus' teaching regarding God is precisely in its emphasis on a loving heavenly Father compared to a less personal Creator more removed from human access. Or as the great Christian writer C. S. Lewis pointed out, grace — undeserved forgiveness and love — is an emphasis uniquely developed in the teachings of Jesus (as in the parable of the Good Samaritan quoted earlier). So I believe that only through exposure to the life and teachings of Jesus do we come to this kind of full understanding of God as a Father of unconditional love.

However, to take this passage and claim that no other understanding or experience of God is meaningful is beyond what I personally can accept or believe. Aside from the very real question of how people who have never heard about Jesus — those born before his time as well as those since his time — could be expected to have this understanding, there is the question of why a given theological formula should be required as normative for all members of the human race regardless of their circumstances or place of birth or cultural background. I believe that the great God of the universe can be revealed in many different circumstances and times.

Indeed, the place and time of our birth clearly will have a major bearing on what we are able to hear and subsequently choose to believe or not believe. For example, simple honesty compels me to say that if I had been born and raised in India, it is likely I would today be a Hindu. However, that same honesty also compels me to say that the life and teachings of Jesus as described in the Gospels have been "saving grace" for me in the sense of constantly challenging me to live in a way that attempts to love God and my neighbor. I am deeply immersed in my own religious tradition and honor it for the way it has helped me live the way I believe God intends. And I so deeply believe in the benefits of knowing this Jesus that I want to share that knowledge with others, even through the writing of this book.

Indeed, I am convinced that Jesus was so uniquely filled with the Spirit of God that I affirm the language used to describe him as the Son of God. I understand this phrase to be a brief way of describing his unique revelation of what God is like, not a phrase to describe a biological relationship. And one of the most helpful ways I have found of answering the question of whether Jesus is God comes from the New Testament historian and scholar N. T. Wright. In one of his short but powerful books, he answers that very provocative question—Is Jesus God?—as follows:

> It's a good question! But the trouble with it is that it's the wrong way round. As historians we know quite a lot about Jesus. We know when he lived and how he died. We know what he taught and the most important things he did. We know something at least of what he believed he had to do, and how he believed he had to do it. But do we know enough about God to be able to complete the equation? When people ask the question, "Is Jesus God?", they tend to assume that we know who *God*

is; the question means, Can you fit Jesus into your God-picture? Well, the best Christian answer has always been: we *don't know,* off the top of our heads, exactly who God is; but we can discover him by looking at Jesus. You could say that at the heart of the Christian faith is the view, not that Jesus is more or less like God, or part of God, but that the being we refer to as "God" was, and is, fully present, and fully discoverable, in and as Jesus of Nazareth.[8]

I have quoted Wright at this point because he says better than I ever could what I mean when I say "Jesus is the Son of God." He has rescued the debate about the relationship of Jesus to God from the biological bent of the Nicene Creed and instead emphasized the significance of Jesus as the revelation of God through "the Word made flesh." But affirming that particular language as useful for myself does not mean that it is my job to judge others who might say it differently, or that I must insist that everyone share my particular understanding regardless of their circumstances or background.

If all this sounds like I have shed a big burden of endless intellectual debate for a simple life of spiritual devotion, read on—and weep or laugh as may be the case. For I will attempt to personalize the beliefs I have gained from the New Testament accounts of the life of Jesus. And most important, I will struggle to understand what it all means for how I should live the rest of my life.

WHAT DIFFERENCE DOES IT MAKE?

8

How Should Faith Shape Our Lives?

Making the transition in belief from a creator God to a personal God is an enormous leap of faith. Nonetheless, I have concluded that the God who created the universe has indeed reached out to us in many ways, but most definitively and understandably in the life of Jesus.

What are the take-home messages from these sources of divine revelation—one shrouded in the mystery of the universe, the other much more understandable in the life of a human being? What specifically do these sources of knowledge say to my mind and heart about how I should live in the midst of the so-called daily grind, the reality of everyday life?

I have personally concluded that there is no better guidance for living than what Jesus taught and how he lived. Probably the most well-known though often least-understood wisdom of Jesus is found in the collected sayings in three long chapters in the Gospel of Matthew, subsequently labeled by Saint Augustine as the Sermon on the Mount. (There is a shorter version of this sermon in the Gospel of Luke.) Many scholars think it unlikely that Jesus actually delivered this whole sermon at one time. More likely, they say, is that Matthew's Gospel pulled together many sayings of Jesus from the oral tradition of the early Jesus Movement and put them into this one passage. Since it is so central to any understanding of Jesus' ethic and message, most of it is reprinted here for those who have never read it. I have omitted parts that might be more difficult to understand without a specific knowledge of the context in which Jesus was speaking. I encourage you to read the entire passage on your own, maybe with a study Bible or commentary to provide background. You will probably find some parts familiar, including the Beatitudes, the Lord's Prayer and the Golden Rule, and other parts more startling, such as the comments on divorce and lust. Some parts you will find almost bizarre. It helps to remember that Jesus often used hyperbole—exaggeration to make a point and therefore not meant to be taken literally, such as cutting off one's hand.

The Sermon starts with the Beatitudes, or "Blessings."

THE SERMON ON THE MOUNT

Now when he saw the crowds, he went up on a mountainside and sat down. His disciples came to him, and he began to teach them, saying:

> *Blessed are the poor in spirit,*
> *for theirs is the kingdom of heaven.*
> *Blessed are those who mourn,*
> *for they will be comforted.*
> *Blessed are the meek,*
> *for they will inherit the earth.*

Blessed are those who hunger and thirst for righteousness,
    for they will be filled.
Blessed are the merciful,
    for they will be shown mercy.
Blessed are the pure in heart,
    for they will see God.
Blessed are the peacemakers,
    for they will be called sons of God.
Blessed are those who are persecuted because of righteousness,
    for theirs is the kingdom of heaven. (Matthew 5:1-10 NIV)

You have heard that it was said to the people long ago, "Do not murder and anyone who murders will be subject to judgment." But I tell you that anyone who is angry with his brother will be subject to judgment. . . .

Therefore, if you are offering your gift at the altar and there remember that your brother has something against you, leave your gift there in front of the altar. First go and be reconciled to your brother; then come and offer your gift. (Matthew 5:21-24 NIV)

You have heard that it was said, "Do not commit adultery." But I tell you that anyone who looks at a woman lustfully has already committed adultery with her in his heart. If your right eye causes you to sin, gouge it out and throw it away. It is better for you to lose one part of your body than for your whole body to be thrown into hell. And if your right hand causes you to sin, cut it off and throw

*it away. It is better for you to lose one part of your body than for
your whole body to go into hell.*

*It has been said, "Anyone who divorces his wife must give her
a certificate of divorce." But I tell you that anyone who divorces
his wife, except for marital unfaithfulness, causes her to become
an adulteress, and anyone who marries the divorced woman
commits adultery.* (Matthew 5:27-32 NIV)

This harsh comment on divorce stands in stark contrast to the
"liberal" interpretation of religious rules operative in parts of Jewish
society at the time. For example, one prominent rabbi taught that a
man could divorce his wife for anything she did to displease him, no
matter how trivial, simply by saying "I divorce you" three times. It
would appear that Jesus was trying to directly oppose such practice.

---

*You have heard that it was said, "Eye for eye, and tooth for
tooth." But I tell you, Do not resist an evil person. If someone
strikes you on the right cheek, turn to him the other also. And if
someone wants to sue you and take your tunic, let him have your
cloak as well. If someone forces you to go one mile, go with him
two miles. Give to the one who asks you, and do not turn away
from the one who wants to borrow from you.*

*You have heard that it was said, "Love your neighbor and hate
your enemy." But I tell you: Love your enemies and pray for those
who persecute you, that you may be sons of your Father in
heaven.* (Matthew 5:38-45)

Be careful not to do your "acts of righteousness" before men, to be seen by them. If you do, you will have no reward from your Father in heaven.

So when you give to the needy, do not announce it with trumpets, as the hypocrites do in the synagogues and on the streets, to be honored by men. I tell you the truth, they have received their reward in full. But when you give to the needy, do not let your left hand know what your right hand is doing, so that your giving may be in secret. Then your Father, who sees what is done in secret, will reward you.

And when you pray, do not be like the hypocrites, for they love to pray standing in the synagogues and on the street corners to be seen by men. I tell you the truth, they have received their reward in full. But when you pray, go into your room, close the door and pray to your Father, who is unseen. Then your Father, who sees what is done in secret, will reward you. And when you pray, do not keep on babbling like pagans, for they think they will be heard because of their many words. Do not be like them, for your Father knows what you need before you ask him.

This, then, is how you should pray:

"Our Father in heaven,
hallowed be your name,
your kingdom come,
your will be done
    on earth as it is in heaven.
Give us today our daily bread.
Forgive us our debts,
    as we also have forgiven our debtors.

And lead us not into temptation,
   but deliver us from the evil one." (Matthew 6:1-13 NIV)

"Do not store up for yourselves treasures on earth, where moth and rust destroy, and where thieves break in and steal. But store up for yourselves treasures in heaven, where moth and rust do not destroy, and where thieves do not break in and steal. For where your treasure is, there your heart will be also. . . .

"No one can serve two masters. Either he will hate the one and love the other, or he will be devoted to the one and despise the other. You cannot serve both God and Money.

"Therefore I tell you, do not worry about your life, what you will eat or drink; or about your body, what you will wear. Is not life more important than food, and the body more important than clothes? Look at the birds of the air; they do not sow or reap or store away in barns, and yet your heavenly Father feeds them. Are you not much more valuable than they? Who of you by worrying can add a single hour to his life? . . .

"But seek first his kingdom and his righteousness, and all these things will be given to you as well. Therefore do not worry about tomorrow, for tomorrow will worry about itself. Each day has enough trouble of its own.

"Do not judge, or you too will be judged. For in the same way you judge others, you will be judged, and with the measure you use, it will be measured to you. . . .

"So in everything, do to others what you would have them do to you, for this sums up the Law and the Prophets. . . .

> "Therefore everyone who hears these words of mine and puts
> them into practice is like a wise man who built his house on the
> rock. The rain came down, the streams rose, and the winds blew
> and beat against that house; yet it did not fall, because it had its
> foundation on the rock. But everyone who hears these words of
> mine and does not put them into practice is like a foolish man
> who built his house on sand. The rain came down, the streams
> rose, and the winds blew and beat against that house, and it fell
> with a great crash."
>
> When Jesus had finished saying these things, the crowds were
> amazed at his teaching, because he taught as one who had au-
> thority, and not as their teachers of the law. (Matthew 6:19-21,
> 24-27, 33-34; 7:1-2, 12, 24-29 NIV)

In most sermons or homilies the preacher makes a few simple
points to give realistic guidance and encouragement for daily living.
In dramatic contrast this sermon not only makes us feel guilty but
takes the wind right out of our moral sails. How can anyone possibly
live like this? And more important, why should we? Doesn't this
"poor in spirit" and "meekness" stuff fly in the face of reality?

In his very provocative insights on the Sermon on the Mount, the
popular religious writer Philip Yancey quotes a British psychologist
from a speech given to the Royal Society of Medicine:

> The spirit of self-sacrifice which permeates Christianity, and is so highly
> prized in the Christian religious life, is masochism moderately indulged.
> A much stronger expression of it is to be found in Christ's teaching in the
> Sermon on the Mount. This blesses the poor, the meek, the persecuted;
> exhorts us not to resist evil but to offer the second cheek to the smiter;

and to do good to them that hate you and forgive men their trespasses. All this breathes masochism.[1]

Yancey also quotes from some college-student essays written in response to a reading of this Sermon:

The stuff the churches preach is extremely strict and allows for almost no fun without thinking it is a sin or not.

It was hard to read and made me feel like I had to be perfect and no one is.

The things asked in this sermon are absurd. To look at a woman is adultery. That is the most extreme, stupid, unhuman [sic] statement that I have ever heard.[2]

At first blush the sophisticated psychologist and the earthy students seem to have a point. So consider the way in which British New Testament scholar J. B. Phillips recasts the Beatitudes with a more "realistic" wisdom (the Greek word for "blessed" can be translated with several words; Phillips uses "happy"):

Happy are the "pushers": for they get on in the world

Happy are the hard-boiled: for they never let life hurt them

Happy are they who complain: for they get their own way in
    the end

Happy are the blasé: for they never worry over their sins

Happy are the slave-drivers: for they get results

Happy are the knowledgeable men of the world: for they know
    their way around.

Happy are the trouble-makers: for they make people take
    notice of them.[3]

Now that feels more like it: the cool, confident, calculating and competitive American way, much more likely to lead to the material fruits of the American dream. Sure, as adults we may preach compassion and consideration to our kids, but our actions all too often send the message that those who push and complain are the ones who actually get ahead in the race of life. But isn't there some nice, safe, comfortable middle ground that could satisfy both the demands of reality in the competitive marketplace and this seemingly unrealistic ethic dramatized in the Sermon on the Mount?

Yes, say some observers of human nature, there is—and it is called compartmentalization. Once again I turn to Scott Peck, who comments on this phenomenon:

> Human beings have a remarkable capacity to take things that are related to each other and stick them in separate airtight compartments so they don't rub up against each other and cause them much pain. We're all familiar with the man who goes to church on Sunday morning, believing that he loves God and God's creation and his fellow human beings, but who, on Monday morning, has no trouble with his company's policy of dumping toxic wastes in the local stream. He can do this because he has religion in one compartment and his business in another. . . . It is a very comfortable way to operate, but integrity it is not. The word *integrity* comes from the same root as *integrate*. It means to achieve wholeness, which is the opposite of compartmentalize. Compartmentalization is easy. Integrity is painful. But without it there can be no wholeness.[4]

Maybe the Sermon on the Mount seems so painful, troublesome and disturbing because it radically indicts our human tendency toward compartmentalization and its ultimate outcome, blatant hypocrisy. Jesus portrays the kind of rigorous honesty that requires us to integrate the demands of the real world with the promptings of our spiritual compass. I believe this kind of wholeness requires that we at least consider how we might live, as described by Jesus in the Sermon, in a manner quite different from the conventional lifestyle of our culture.

I realize this all sounds very theoretical. So at this point I want to attempt applying some of the themes of the Sermon on the Mount (which are very consistent with the way Jesus taught and acted throughout his own life) to a real human life—the one I know best, my own. This is where the theoretical rubber of spiritual speculation meets the rough road of life. In my case this means wrestling with how to apply these principles (also illustrated in the parables and episodes from the life of Jesus described in section two) to my everyday life. It would be hypocritical of me *not* to do so if I really believe, as I do, that Jesus modeled and taught the kind of life that the creator God has in mind for us.

In fact, I have been trying to follow these ideals throughout my adult life but with great difficulty. Now that I have passed my sixty-fifth birthday, I feel a special urgency about the choices I should be making. I will focus on a few key areas of daily living illumined by the probing light of the Sermon on the Mount.

ALL OF GOD'S CHILDREN

My favorite Sunday school song was "Jesus loves the little children, all the children of the world. Red and yellow, black and white, they are precious in his sight. Jesus loves the little children of the world." However politically incorrect it may be now, in childhood I loved that song because I knew it included me. I was one of the white ones, and even though I had very little contact growing up in Rockford with black, yellow and red children, I somehow knew that there were a lot of different kinds of children in our world—and I had absolutely no doubt that God loved them all as much as me.

Most of that absolute conviction came from observing my mother, a woman who radiated the love of God to everyone she knew, not so much with words but simply and profoundly in the way she treated all people. After my mother died, many people told me, "Your mother didn't have an enemy in the world." As I grew older I realized that I never heard my mother say an unkind word about anyone. She was not simpleminded or Pollyanna-ish; she would comment on how the difficult circumstances of people's lives sometimes caused them to act in hurtful ways. But she was always kind, even to those who didn't deserve her warmth—*especially* to those who didn't deserve it. She was an incredible role model and her example is indelible. Of course, this was all too good to be true. Or was it? As I went off to college and medical school, I quickly saw other role models in action—from intellectually arrogant professors who delighted in putting down lesser minds, to professionally arrogant physicians and journalists who often treated those lower on the ladder with rudeness, even contempt. But isn't that what is needed to "get ahead" and "get things done" and "accomplish personal goals" and "climb the ladder of success"?

Obviously, it depends on what we mean by *success*. If it means a list of achievements that can be measured by academic titles and degrees or societal recognition or financial fortune, then treating other people as means to our ends can be helpful, at least in the short run. But what about the long run, the totality of our lives as they will be evaluated at the finish line? I believe that Jesus, and other holy people like him, really did have it right when it comes to the Golden Rule, that what he teaches is good because it is true. It is true because in the longer run the way we treat people will usually come back to heal or haunt us.

In the very long run the way we have treated people, including those closest to us, will be very much with us at the finish line—where little else will matter. Indeed, in the many times I have been with people in the "valley of the shadow of death," I have never heard them wish they had accumulated more money, attained more recognition or spent more time in passing pleasure. But I have heard many regrets about missed opportunities to be with loved ones in truly meaningful ways. This kind of living takes thought and sometimes hard work, especially if you are not blessed with the right kind of role models growing up—or the right kind of happiness and contentment genes. (I fully expect that someday we will understand a very specific contribution from our genetic makeup to these kinds of personality traits.)

I believe we can overcome difficult childhoods and chromosomes, at least in part, by consciously working at seeing all people as children of God and therefore deserving of decent and humane treatment. Personally, I have found two resources invaluable in that effort. The first is a group of close friends, most (but not all) of whom I have known since childhood or adolescence. The single criterion they have in common is that they love me for who I am, not for what I have accomplished. This, of course, should be the hallmark of parental love—so-called unconditional love. Theologians love to say it is the kind of love shown by God and taught by Jesus during his earthly life (in such parables as the prodigal son). That kind of love can never be fully achieved in human life, but apart from family, the support of true friends comes closest. And beside the sheer joy they bring to my life, these friends perform one very important task for me: they call attention to sprouts of excessive ego without destroying its honorable essence. I have come to believe these friendships are literally worth their weight in gold, and I work at cultivating them to keep them a vital part of my life.

The other inspiration I have found invaluable consists of people outside my professional and work circles. Understandably, we tend to spend most of our time with those in our own social and career circles. (This raises the important question of how, for example, doctors and journalists — the two professional groups I know best — can really be "healers" or "truth-tellers" if we spend most of our time with like-minded and well-circumstanced people, and therefore have little practical experience with the many others less fortunate in our world.) For me, one of the most important correctives to this tendency has been a local church, to which I have always belonged, wherever I have lived — people who accept me as a fellow traveler in the journey of faith and not as a TV personality or well-known physician. These communities of faith — people of all walks sharing the common struggle to find meaning in our world — have ministered to me in many ways, but most importantly in helping me to focus on the Way taught and modeled by Jesus. Together we have tried to understand how to apply that way to our present lives.

Another very important pathway for this kind of corrective in my life comes through the many phone calls I receive from people often desperate for advice in figuring out their medical problems. Some of these calls come from my colleagues or close friends. But many more come from people I don't know, through referral from family or friends or just out of the blue. I confess there are times when I dread taking another call because I know it will mean time I supposedly don't have and a weariness of spirit that comes from listening to often tragic stories. But I have made it a matter of spiritual discipline to take these calls and help as I can—and invariably I am the one who is helped and blessed by the spirit of "those who mourn." Indeed, through interacting with people who are meek and merciful, who hunger and thirst for righteousness, who are peacemakers, I most often observe the wholeness and health possible only when we understand our own shortcomings and see all people as children of the same Creator. What a different world we would have if we could all see each other as children of God!

Probably the most infamous passage in the Sermon on the Mount is the one that then-presidential candidate Jimmy Carter referred to in a *Playboy* magazine interview—"anyone who looks at a woman lustfully has already committed adultery with her in his heart" (certainly this is a unisex statement which cuts both ways). Did Jesus say this to make us all hopelessly guilt-ridden about our normal sexual drives and instincts—an attitude that unfortunately has been amplified by too many Puritan moralists down through the years? There is no evidence from Jesus' real-life encounters with both men and women that this was his usual practice. Rather, I believe this is simply one more example of the radical nature of Jesus' vision for the way God intends us to treat each other—not as "objects" to be used for selfish purposes (in this case, sexual) but rather as persons of worth, equally valued in the sight of God. It is this message that saturates Jesus' life and teachings, a message that is at the heart of spiritual "tough love"—meaning the kind of respect we should show toward everyone even when we don't naturally feel like it, even to those who appear to be our enemies.

ALL OF GOD'S TALENT

A superficial reading of the Sermon on the Mount could lead to the conclusion that we should throw ourselves on the mercy of God and do nothing for ourselves. I have known religious fanatics (as they are usually sarcastically described) who have done just that: gone out naively on some apparently unwise mission in the name of God, trusting that "God will provide." Sometimes it works; sometimes it doesn't. But is that what Jesus really had in mind when he counseled us not to worry about tomorrow, for "tomorrow will worry about itself"? I personally don't believe so, because there are many other teachings from Jesus in the New Testament that clearly counsel the wise use of time and talent. For example, consider the parable of the talents.

THE PARABLE OF THE TALENTS

Again, [the kingdom of heaven] will be like a man going on a journey, who called his servants and entrusted his property to them. To one he gave five talents of money, to another two talents, and to another one talent, each according to his ability. Then he went on his journey. The man who had received the five talents went at once and put his money to work and gained five more. So also, the one with the two talents gained two more. But the man who had received the one talent went off, dug a hole in the ground and hid his master's money.

After a long time the master of those servants returned and settled accounts with them. The man who had received the five talents brought the other five. "Master," he said, "you entrusted me with five talents. See, I have gained five more."

His master replied, "Well done, good and faithful servant! You have been faithful with a few things; I will put you in charge of many things. Come and share your master's happiness!"

The man with the two talents also came. "Master," he said, "you entrusted me with two talents; see, I have gained two more."

His master replied, "Well done, good and faithful servant! You have been faithful with a few things; I will put you in charge of many things. Come and share your master's happiness."

Then the man who had received the one talent came. "Master," he said, "I knew that you are a hard man, harvesting where you have not sown and gathering where you have not scattered seed. So I was afraid and went out and hid your talent in the ground. See, here is what belongs to you."

His master replied, "You wicked, lazy servant! So you knew that I harvest where I have not sown and gather where I have not scattered seed? Well, then, you should have put my money on deposit with the bankers, so that when I returned I would have received it back with interest.

"Take the talent from him and give it to the one who has the ten talents. For everyone who has will be given more, and he will have an abundance. Whoever does not have, even what he has will be taken from him. And throw that worthless servant outside,

> *into the darkness, where there will be weeping and gnashing of*
> *teeth.*" (Matthew 25:14-30 NIV)

A word of caution about parables: scholars agree that they are told to make one major overall point, not as stories to be applied to real life in every possible detail. For example, it would be a mistake to take this parable as an endorsement of putting our money in the bank to earn interest or treating those with lesser talent as lesser human beings. Rather, the obvious point of this parable is the importance of using and developing whatever resources we have. I have come to believe that one important way we can discover the "will of God" for ourselves is through the talents we are born with. This is why I have always believed that the best possible plan for any life is to discover what we really enjoy or are good at (in my experience, the two are almost always the same) and go for it, regardless of the status or income such activity might provide. Of course, that is not always possible. But when it is, it's the way to go.

There are, however, two "talents" that virtually all of us receive by virtue of membership in the human race, gifts we can use wisely or foolishly—the gifts of time and the human body. I am not going to dwell on the importance of time; we all know how precious and how easily wasted it is. But my experience as a physician has dramatically demonstrated how often we take for granted the gift of our body. Perhaps one of the best benefits from belief in God is understanding the body's sacredness. I recall a conversation with media friends in which talk turned to the use of drugs in their younger years. Various people described their adventures with mind-altering substances— some to great laughter, others to gasps of horror. When it came my turn, I became red-faced describing how I grew up in a family and church who viewed the body as, in the words of the apostle Paul, "the temple of the Holy Spirit," meaning that it was wrong to do things to your body that might harm it. Well, as you can imagine, there was stunned silence in the room. Nobody knew what to say, including me. Then someone murmured, "I wish I'd been brought up that way—it would have saved a lot of grief."

Today, we know that religious lifestyles correlate statistically with better health and longer life, for reasons such as a reduced chance of using dangerous drugs, including alcohol and tobacco. (I have chosen not to write about this important subject in this book because so many others have already done so—see the "Suggested Reading" list.) Unfortunately, some religious views border on fanaticism, teaching that all pleasure is wrong. But there is much to be said for regarding the body as a gift, as a "talent" that needs to be nurtured and respected.

ALL OF GOD'S MONEY

When I graduated from seminary and got married, Nancy and I expected that I would work as a parish minister, and therefore we anticipated living a life of meager financial means. But in following a path that allowed me to nurture my talents further, I found myself earning much more than I ever expected. Today, with considerably more than meager means, we are in the spiritually awkward position of having far more than we truly need for necessities. What should we do?

The teachings of Jesus are all too clear: although money itself is not evil and can be a tool for good, the love of money can clearly be evil. According to the Sermon on the Mount we should give most of it away and keep only enough for necessities. But we have two homes, two cars (plus one for each of our children), many coats and too many shoes! We have more money in the bank than we will ever need for basic necessities. What should we do?

What Nancy and I have done so far is to practice a discipline of giving a fixed percentage of our gross income to church and charity. In recent years we have usually given away more than that, and I meet with a good friend every year to exchange tax returns in order to encourage each other to give more. We have arranged our will so that the majority of our savings will eventually go to charity rather than to our children, though they will certainly receive enough for significant help as they plan their futures.

However, what Nancy and I have *not* done so far is give until it hurts, not even close. We have not suffered the pangs of poverty, ever, and we have not had to worry about necessities. So are we even close to using money the way Jesus taught we should?

The answer is plainly no. And quite frankly, I don't know what to do about it—yet. We are contemplating some fairly radical changes, which would include cutting down on the oversupply of luxuries and giving the difference to those in true need. I have a growing conviction that it is not right for me to live as well as I now do. But what about the argument that I have earned it—that I have worked hard (which is true) and at least sometimes have used my talents for some common good (which is also true)? Deep in my heart I also know how much of my good fortune has been way beyond my control and effort—such as having been born in this particular country, having loving and supportive parents, and being genetically blessed with good physical and mental health. These are invaluable gifts for which I can take no personal credit. Indeed, the seemingly serendipitous distribution of the world's goods and the resulting suffering disturb me deeply precisely because it often seems to be so much a matter of luck. So when I hear talk about how we deserve what we have received, I become very uneasy because I know there is much more to my good fortune than such talk recognizes. And that leads me to the most difficult and mysterious of all the topics I have tried to cover so far.

Why have I had such good fortune while others have had such tragedy? Why do some people suffer great misfortune, without seeming to have God's protection or intervention? If God intends for us to live in certain ways, then it would follow that we should all start off on equal footing. Yet life seems randomly cruel to some and kind to others. What difference does it make what we believe about God's involvement or lack thereof in our lives? As a way of wrestling with these questions, I will tell you a very personal love story—how Nancy and I adopted our son, Nolden.

9

IS GOD IN CONTROL?

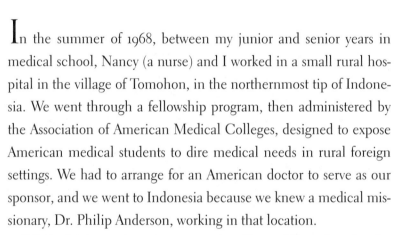

In the summer of 1968, between my junior and senior years in medical school, Nancy (a nurse) and I worked in a small rural hospital in the village of Tomohon, in the northernmost tip of Indonesia. We went through a fellowship program, then administered by the Association of American Medical Colleges, designed to expose American medical students to dire medical needs in rural foreign settings. We had to arrange for an American doctor to serve as our sponsor, and we went to Indonesia because we knew a medical missionary, Dr. Philip Anderson, working in that location.

While driving us into the mountain village of Tomohon for the first time, Dr. Anderson joked that he had a little Indonesian child picked out for us. We laughed because nothing could have been more improbable; I faced several more years of training, and we were neither emotionally nor financially ready to start a family.

I soon met the little eighteen-month-old boy Dr. Anderson had in mind, because he was still in the "pediatric ward" (meaning wooden slats on a cement floor) after being left at the hospital by a "family friend." He had some minor problems that needed attention but was basically in good health. After several weeks of getting to know him during my hospital work, I impulsively decided to take him with me to a birthday party for one of the Indonesian nurses. Nancy had been working in another part of the hospital, so that evening she met him for the first time. After the party we decided to take the toddler back to our quarters and give him a bath. (He was quite dirty because he ran around the hospital compound without clothes most of the time.) When the time came for him to go back to the hospital, we decided he should at least spend the night with us; I would take him back with me in the morning. We had a wonderful evening playing with him.

The next morning over breakfast, we looked at each other and immediately decided we should adopt this totally lovable young boy so he wouldn't have to go into the orphanage when he was released from the hospital. From that moment on he was our son just as surely as if he had been born to us.

There is more to the story. After Nolden had been living with us for several weeks, a teenage girl showed up one day to check up on him, and we quickly learned that she was his mother. She told us how the father had left her when Nolden was born, how she had raised him for the first eighteen months of his life as long as she could breast-feed him, and how she had brought him back to the father when she could no longer afford to take care of him. The father, posing as a family friend, had brought him to the hospital. All the while our hearts were pounding in fear that she would now want him back.

We explained to the young mother what had happened and how much we wanted to adopt the boy and take him back to America with us. To her great credit, in our eyes, she readily agreed that this would be the best plan for him since she was in no position to raise a child. And so we were allowed to keep this great gift that had so unexpectedly come into our lives.

I could go on and on about the events that followed—the enormous difficulties we encountered in trying to get U.S. Immigration Service approval for bringing him back with us, the very real threat of having to leave Nancy behind to take care of him when I returned to medical school, the immigration officer in Alaska who allowed him into the country even though his status was not fully legal and so on. But the bottom line is that we returned to medical school in the fall with a young son who has turned out to be one of the great joys in our life. As I write this, Nolden is in his mid-thirties, a graduate of the Rhode Island School of Design, a freelance furniture designer and married to a young woman who is also adopted. A few years ago they welcomed their first child—our first grandchild![1]

DOES GOD CAUSE GOOD THINGS TO HAPPEN?

I tell this story to raise the very complicated and profound question of whether or not it's possible and wise to believe in "providence"— the idea that the God responsible for the creation of this universe might also "arrange" or "direct" human affairs in everyday ways. In this context, is there any reason to believe that somehow God "arranged" that we would meet and adopt Nolden?

In retrospect it's often startling to see how events in our lives that at the time appeared to be totally disconnected seem to have stunning—even spooky—connections. For example, in the case of our son's adoption, Nancy and I could conceivably trace a line from the seemingly chance events of being raised in the same church denomination (though geographically separated by a thousand miles), meeting in Chicago because of that connection (she in nurses' training at the hospital sponsored by our church, I attending their seminary), falling in love and getting married, my surprising decision to attend medical school, which led to the fellowship program, placing us in Indonesia because we knew a doctor who would sponsor us, arriving just at the time Nolden had been abandoned at the hospital. *What a stretch*, you might say! And I would agree, from the point of view that sees all of life as a series of entirely accidental and unrelated events. But what about a perspective that views life as a series of choices which, when made according to a set of principles based on maximizing the love of God and neighbor, may over time increase the possibility of ending up with a more fulfilling life? I know that also sounds like a stretch. But as I look back on my own life and choices, I can discern that kind of providential principle in my life and in the lives of others I know well. Put another way, *the many individual choices we make along the way start to build up in a collective direction that can ultimately make a dramatic difference, depending on those individual choices.*

I should make clear that I am not suggesting something as rigid or simplistic as "if I had not met Nancy my life would have been doomed," or "if we had not gone to Indonesia, Nolden's life would have been ruined." I believe that there are many opportunities for all of us to make good choices, and if one does not work out, another will come along. Nor do I mean to suggest that even if we attempt to make good choices, everything will turn out OK. Life is too full of freedom and mystery for that guarantee. But I *am* trying to say that over a lifetime, if we make choices according to standards suggested by the Sermon on the Mount, we at least increase our potential for experiencing personal contentment, of being blessed.

And if that kind of "probability pattern" is built into the fabric of human affairs, in which different choices have different consequences, might we not legitimately call it "providence" and see it as part of God's creative design? I readily admit this concept is not the kind of providence that many religious people adhere to—that is, God constantly directing the detailed traffic of everyday human affairs. But for me this "providence of probability" makes much more sense because it acknowledges the very real freedom—permitting free choice, but with consequences—we humans are allowed by the creator God. In other words I believe God has designed our world in a way that allows us to become partners with God in helping to determine the outcomes of our lives. We are not puppets at the ends of cosmic strings attached to the fingers of God. Rather we are like athletes, in this case entered in the race of life itself, who must make choices about how to use (or abuse) those gifts and opportunities we have been given.

Put another way, *when we make important life choices based on purely selfish considerations, we eventually find ourselves "rewarded" for such choices.* As C. S. Lewis put it in *The Great Divorce*, "There are only two kinds of people in the end: those who say to God, 'Thy will be done,' and those to whom God says, in the end, '*Thy* will be done.' "[2] Even though there may be no immediate consequence of each individual choice we make, there will be an ultimate and cumulative effect from the many choices we make in our lives. We may be rich and famous but unhappy and unfulfilled precisely because we have ended up with what we have been choosing. Similarly, when we make choices according to the "will of God"—which, according to Jesus, means to love God and our neighbors as ourselves—we are more likely to end up with fewer material rewards but considerably more personal satisfaction and contentment. Because I believe these consequences are built into the way God created this world, I call them "providential"—intended by God but resulting from our free choices.

However, any concept of providence can be distorted. For example, what are we to make of the many wartime claims that "God is on our side"? We have heard such claims from both sides in most past wars, and we hear them today about conflicts in the Middle East. Sometimes it seems obvious that there is a specific evil—or a specifically evil person—that needs to be confronted and eliminated. For example, very few people would argue today about the necessity of removing Hitler and his cohorts from power on the world stage. But even when the legitimacy of war seems clear, I cringe at the religious language so often used to justify the actual destruction and killing—namely, that it's God's will.

Jesus reveals a God who weeps over the loss of life, even when justified by earthly necessity, because it represents a failure of the gift of free choice. In other words, war is always a failure of some humans to choose life over death, to choose love over hatred, to choose inclusion over exclusion. Although I believe war sometimes becomes necessary to correct the results of our human sinfulness, I can't believe it is ever God's hope for humankind.

And I become particularly upset when I hear people talk about the safe return of loved ones from war as the result of God's direct action that by implication resulted in the death of others. During

World War II a popular book came out titled *God Is My Co-pilot*. Commenting on that idea in the context of his thirty-five combat missions in a B-24 during WWII, George McGovern recently wrote, "I give thanks to God for our survival, but somehow I could never quite picture God sitting at the controls of a bomber or squinting through a bombsight deciding which of his creatures should survive and which should die. It did not simplify matters theologically when Sam Adams, my navigator—and easily the godliest man on my ten-member crew—was killed in action early in the war. He was planning to become a clergyman at war's end."[3]

At an utterly trivial level by contrast, I also cringe when I hear God's name invoked as the author of victory on the athletic field, implying that God arranged the defeat of the opponent; or I hear God invoked as the author of victory in business competition, once again implying that God is the reason for someone else's loss. My reading of the Gospels suggests that God wants all his creatures to "win" in terms of life fulfillment and no one to "lose" in the game of life.

WHY DOESN'T GOD PREVENT BAD THINGS FROM HAPPENING?

When I was a child, both the starry heaven above and the Bible stories my mother read to me seemed to convey a very simple and consistent message: God, the Creator of the entire universe, loved me, little Timmy Johnson in Rockford, Illinois. Not only that but this God had provided me with all the blessings around me: loving parents, a safe home, food and clothing, friends to play with, trips to take to nearby lakes and parks. Believe it or not, and I am truly embarrassed now to admit this, it really wasn't until I went to college in the big city of Chicago that I began to understand more fully that life wasn't quite that simple or lovely for many people, maybe even most people. The questions about suffering and inequities and actual evil started coming at me—first from books and then from real life. When I became a medical student, I began to see life truly in the raw, both physically and emotionally. How could I still believe in the God of my childhood, the One who provides for our every need, when there was such horrible suffering in the world?

Let's readily admit that much human suffering can be attributed to the immoral choices made by individuals, organizations and authority structures such as governments. But that still leaves an enormous amount of suffering that cannot be so explained: natural disasters and tragic diseases beyond our control. This issue is usually referred to as the problem of "undeserved suffering," which we confront in trying to reconcile belief in a loving and just Creator with the terrible events in human life that do not result from the consequences of human choice. Why wouldn't such a God prevent meaningless, cruel and evil events from taking place? The conventional religious explanation for this kind of suffering is that it is the "price we must pay" for the greater benefit of the true freedom in the universe allowed by God, a freedom that must also pervade nature if it is to be total freedom. There are other traditional responses to this problem, but rather than try to summarize them here I will point you to several of the many thoughtful books on this subject (see "Suggested Reading").

For many, the problem of undeserved suffering is the major stumbling block to belief in God. I could easily devote this entire chapter to wrestling with it, but I would rather not attempt in brief, less-than-adequate fashion what others have already done in much more depth. However, even though I can't articulate a fully satisfying answer to this age-old question, I can insist that there *might* be an answer. Just because no one who has taken on this question has come up with a fully satisfactory answer doesn't mean there isn't one. It is similar to the conundrum we encounter in studying the physical universe: just because we cannot explain it all doesn't mean there isn't an explanation. So it is also, I think, with the "moral universe."

At this point I will describe what is for me the most helpful way to approach this terrible dilemma—namely, the age-old exercise of trying to "play God" and come up with an alternative to the world we now have. Though it sounds arrogant even to suggest alternatives to the universe as is, it's only fair to try if I am willing to complain about the present one. But every time I try to do so, I end up admitting that I can't imagine a world any different than the one we know. Certainly, when I contemplate the unimaginable sufferings of so many in our world, I would readily vote for a world without any suffering. Yet when I think more logically rather than simply voting with my heart, I find such a possible world less appealing than it first might appear. For example, imagining a world with neither suffering nor death (the ultimate cause of human uncertainty and anxiety) also conjures up a world in which humans would be incredibly smug, pursuing life without worry or concern.

So I find myself torn between the natural desire for a world without suffering, where we would feast forever on a cosmic silver platter, and the present one, where there is at least the possibility of striving to overcome pain and suffering with honest love and real choice. Does this mean that I can conclude—with some previous thinkers on this subject—that even with all its problems, this world is, after all is said and done, the "best of all possible worlds"? No, that is not what I mean or conclude. It may indeed be the best of all possible worlds *that I can imagine with my limitations as a human being*. But I would hope that the God who (I believe) created this universe has a bigger and better plan in mind than what I see so far.

In other words, if I can't believe there is more to the created universe than what I now perceive in this journey we call human life, then I am the first to admit my disappointment with the "plan of God" as I have been exposed to it thus far. Put another way, if I can't believe in some future existence beyond the earthly journey we experience from birth to death, then I must reluctantly conclude that God did not get it right, at least this time. Put still another way, the present world of earthly existence is at times so unfair—*and there is simply no other way to describe the suffering of innocent human beings and even innocent animals*—that it cries out for ultimate justice. And if that does not happen in this earthly existence—which it clearly does not in too many cases—then I believe it must happen in some future time if there is a God of justice and love, which is the only kind of God I care to believe in. This brings me to the issue of life after death, the ultimate question of whether God is truly in control of what happens to us.

IS THERE LIFE AFTER DEATH?

I believe in life after death, but I don't know it to be a fact in the same way I can verify something through scientific experiment. Unlike some who claim to have had visions during near-death experiences or encounters with people who have died, I have never had such moments. However, I have talked to people who have described such experiences so vividly that I am inclined to believe them. For example, here is an event described to me by a very rational, intelligent and (at the time) nonreligious person who with her sister had returned to a motel room from the bedside of their dying father. She described what happened while her sister fell asleep and she lay awake in bed:

> All of a sudden, my father's hospital room appeared in the motel room before my eyes so real I felt I could touch it—as real as anything in real life. The room was as we had left it a few hours before with my father in the bed as we had left him, still living. All of a sudden, my mother, who had been dead for many years, appeared at his bedside and held out her hand to him as though she was assisting him from the bed. And then the scene faded.[4]

You have probably already guessed the rest of her story—the phone call that came from the hospital shortly after, telling her that her father had died at the exact time the vision had appeared. So real was the experience that it transformed this person's life to one of religious practice (in the Episcopal church) and to a very strong belief in life after death, with an almost total absence of any fear of death.

It is very tempting to dismiss this—and other similar descriptions—as nothing more than wishful thinking. But what impresses me about at least some of them is how utterly unexpected and surprising they were and how intensely real they seemed. Obviously, these kinds of experiences do not prove life after death in any acceptable scientific sense. But for me they do hint at the possibility of some kind of continuing identity beyond the death of our earthly body. This possibility does not seem outrageous, given what we have learned about the nature of physical reality, which could easily allow for continuing "identities" far different from what we know as the earthly body of a human being. Add to this the experiences of mystics and the momentary flashes of strange, "other-worldly" intuitions some have experienced, and it all seems at least to raise possibilities beyond the physical life span of earthly existence.

But as I said above (and along with the teachings of Jesus regarding eternal life), for me the most convincing "argument" for the probability of existence beyond human life is the tug of unfinished business in this earthly pilgrimage—the very real sense of injustice that needs to be corrected, of suffering that needs to be explained or compensated. Those kinds of unfinished business tilt me in the direction of "more to come" rather than "this is all there is." Again, I acknowledge this kind of yearning could be nothing more than wishful thinking. It is a leaning, not a scientific certainty. But it is a bet I am willing to make, and that brings me to one of the most famous religious wagers of all time, proposed by the same Blaise Pascal we met in section one.

PASCAL'S WAGER

The best known of Pascal's *Pensées* is probably his wager—basically a bet he suggests for those skeptical about the existence of God. Pascal puts his thesis very bluntly: "*Let us weigh up the gain and the loss involved in calling heads that God exists. Let us assess the two cases: if you win you win everything, if you lose you lose nothing.*"[5] But, you might say, you lose your integrity and self-respect if you bet on God without really believing it. For that reason, I personally don't feel comfortable with this kind of intellectual bet—a logical analysis that concludes "there is nothing to lose" in betting that God exists. But I do think there is another kind of spiritual bet that is worth considering, especially when enigmas such as human freedom, divine providence and unjust suffering leave us with a paradoxical tension of yes and no answers to the question of whether God is truly in control. This bet comes down to what we believe about the character of God.

10

CAN WE BET ON
THE HEART OF GOD?

In my experience, finding God in the questions does not mean finding complete answers. In fact, you may discover that along the path of faith, you pick up more questions than you started with. But you might also discover that you need fewer answers, and those you *do* find are enough to live on.

The questions that won't go away can be hard to live with unless you have a way of making peace with uncertainty. Ultimately, I think the only resting place for mysteries of faith lies in a willingness to try to live according to the Way of Jesus. That's why I am raising the final question in this book of what it might mean to "bet on the heart of God."

Once again I turn to a parable of Jesus, this one recorded in the Gospel of Matthew. (Again, remember that Jesus often used symbolic language that was not meant to be taken literally.) This particular story, which has been tagged "The Final Judgment," is a vortex for many of the big questions of belief—salvation, eternal destiny, individual choices, how God views our lives. Perhaps by looking at "the end," we will have a better way of coming back to "the now" and focusing our lives on what matters most.

———❖———

THE PARABLE OF THE FINAL JUDGMENT

When the Son of Man comes as King and all the angels with him, he will sit on his royal throne, and the people of all the nations will be gathered before him. Then he will divide them into two groups, just as a shepherd separates the sheep from the goats. He will put the righteous people at his right and the others at his left.

Then the King will say to the people on his right, "Come you that are blessed by my Father! Come and possess the kingdom which has been prepared for you ever since the creation of the world. I was hungry and you fed me, thirsty and you gave me a drink; I was a stranger and you received me in your homes, naked and you clothed me; I was sick and you took care of me, in prison and you visited me."

The righteous will then answer him, "When, Lord, did we ever see you hungry and feed you or thirsty and give you a drink? When did we ever see you a stranger and welcome you in our homes, or naked and clothe you? When did we ever see you sick or in prison, and visit you?"

The King will reply, "I tell you, whenever you did this for one of the least important of these brothers of mine, you did it for me!"

Then he will say to those on his left, "Away from me, you that are under God's curse! Away to the eternal fire which has been prepared for the Devil and his angels! I was hungry but you would not feed, thirsty but you would not give me a drink; I was a stranger but you would not welcome me in your homes, naked but you would not clothe me; I was sick and in prison but you would not take care of me."

Then they will answer him, "When, Lord, did we ever see you hungry or thirsty or a stranger or naked or sick or in prison, and we would not help you?" The King will reply, "I tell you, whenever you refused to help one of these least important ones, you refused to help me." (Matthew 25:31-45)

Part of the pleasure of reading a novel lies in not knowing how it will turn out until we get to the last page — and then thinking back to how the characters might have lived differently had they known what the end would be like. But real life has an urgency so different from fiction; at the end, it cannot be changed! As the great novelist Franz Kafka reportedly said, "The meaning of life is that it stops."[1] I think he meant that we will never figure out how we should live our life unless we fully understand the significance of the fact that it will end. And then what?

According to this description of final judgment by Jesus, most of us will be in for a big surprise. And most surprising in his description of judgment are the criteria, the standards, the rules of life by which we will be assessed. Jesus' checklist is truly startling when you look at what is *left out*, in contrast to the dominant emphases of so much modern religious teaching.

Notice that there is **no mention of correct thinking.** If you listen to the loud teachings of some Christians, you would think the most important spiritual issues are intellectual — learning the fundamentals of Christianity in the right way, believing the creeds of Christianity in "correct" fashion, quoting the "right" Bible verses to support your views. But Jesus says nothing about these matters of the mind in his portrait of final judgment.

Notice that there is **no mention of correct positions on social or political issues.** The loud discussions in some churches and political circles can make you think that certain conclusions about abortion, homosexuality or the proper place of women are key to becoming a proper follower of Jesus. But Jesus says nothing about these matters of society and morals in his portrait of final judgment—or for that matter, in *any* of his statements as recorded in the Gospels!

Notice that there is **no mention of power or fame or wealth.** If you were to listen to the loud praises of modern society, even in many religious institutions, you would think that what is really important in life are such matters as net worth, educational achievements, memberships in certain clubs, face time on television or print space in newspapers. But Jesus says nothing about these matters of celebrity in his portrait of final judgment.

Finally, notice that there is **no mention of time spent in traditional religious practices.** Based on the loud advice of some religious leaders, you might conclude that time spent in prayer, religious work, Bible study and church participation was the most important. But Jesus says nothing about these matters of religion in his portrait of final judgment.

This is not to say that any or all of these are not important—but apparently they were not the most important to Jesus as he focused on how we will ultimately be judged. If we take the message of this parable at face value, according to Jesus the kind of activity that *will* keep us from being a goat on judgment day is crystal clear—namely, attention to the "least important ones." Obviously these people were very important to Jesus, but he knew—as we all do if we are honest—that they are usually not very important to us. No wonder these ancient words are still so disturbing. Listen to the comments of Dorothy Day, the modern-day saint who founded the Catholic Worker Movement, about this parable: "If we hadn't got Christ's own words for it, it would seem raving lunacy to believe that if I offer a bed and food and hospitality to some man or woman or child . . . that my guest is Christ. There is nothing to show it, perhaps. There are no halos already glowing round their heads—at least none that human eyes can see."[2]

Father Hesburgh, president emeritus of Notre Dame, once said of Dorothy Day that she comforted the afflicted and afflicted the comfortable.[3] Indeed, it is difficult to label the Gospel words regarding final judgment as "good news" given the way most of us live and our conventional priorities. But at least we know how the plot turns out before our story ends.

Actually, we shouldn't be surprised at Jesus' description of final judgment, because his entire life and teachings point to this bottom line: if we really want to live according to the law of the universe and honor God by following the great commandment to love God and our neighbor, then we must be willing to live our lives in service to others, especially to those who are the least among us—the sick, those in prison or in need of food and water and clothes, the strangers who need to be invited into our lives.

But are we meant to do this literally? In other words, can't we be good enough just by taking care of our own—by being good parents, good employers, good workers, good friends? Do we really have to go out of our way to help those who are "strangers"?

This is a tough one for me. I can very easily rationalize that just by doing a good job in my work and by giving significant amounts of my earnings to worthy causes, I have discharged my responsibility to "the least among us." But I am increasingly convinced that is not enough—that if I am to be true to the heart of God, I must discipline myself to be available in a more personal way to those in need.

One person who has taught me this most directly is my daughter, Kiplee. She was born to us three years after we returned from Indonesia with Nolden. From the start she had a mind and will of her own. Somewhat predictably, this independent streak pushed her to do things that sometimes made me anxious and even angry. She barely graduated from high school, went off with some friends to work in San Francisco and eventually decided she needed further education. However, she has now graduated from college (with honors) and has completed a doctoral program in physical therapy.

But here is what really impresses me. For many summers during her vacation, she has volunteered at a camp for people with serious physical or mental challenges. For one month, twenty-four hours a day, she lived with them so they could have a summer camping experience. She fed them, clothed them, bathed them and helped them go to the bathroom. She would come home at the end of the month emotionally and physically exhausted. (For several summers she even went to Mexico after the first camp to help in a similar camp there.) She was doing something I cannot do—actually giving her whole self to those in need. And even though she is not formally religious, I believe she is more in tune with the heart of God than many people I know because she is willing to be available in a total way to those in need.

"Betting on the heart of God" should be more than vague spirituality. As much as possible it should be an informed bet because the stakes are so high. And as you know by now, I believe that the life and teachings of Jesus offer the best information we have about the heart of God. This brings me to the decision point we must all confront once we have been exposed to the life and teachings of Jesus: how do I react to these incredibly difficult and demanding standards put forth by Jesus in the Sermon on the Mount—and in the portrait of final judgment?

One response is boldly stated by a new friend who wrote the following to me: "I hate the Sermon on the Mount. Why? It defeats me. It is too much. I can't even come close to living up to that standard. Likewise, I hate thinking of Jesus as an example for all the same reasons. I just can't do it. I am so far away from meeting that standard that I might as well not even try."

I totally understand and identify with those feelings—because I have them every day of my life when I think about how far I fall short in attempting to be a follower of Jesus. I constantly ask myself two interrelated questions: Did Jesus really believe that the way of life described in the beatitudes would work for his followers in the everyday life of the real world? If so, how could he really expect them to "pull it off" given his firsthand knowledge of how obviously fallible and feeble they really were?

First let's address the question of whether it makes any sense to think about living according to such standards. Actually, I believe that attempting to live according to the Sermon on the Mount is ultimately more healthy and "whole-some" than our usual human practice. I'd like to illustrate this startling suggestion with observations from two sides of the same coin.

The first observation is simply a reminder of what we know all too well: *the typical practices and mores of our secular world have not resulted in a planet full of happy, fulfilled and contented human beings.* I won't waste your time by listing all the evidence: the barrage of movies, music, TV reports, tabloids and Internet sources spew out more stories about tragic lives ruined by drugs, promiscuity and violence than we can possibly absorb. Clearly, the enormous freedom and wealth that permeates much of our "advanced" and "enlightened" society has not produced for most of us what presumably we all long for—a sense of fulfillment and contentment about who we are and what we do.

The second observation is far less apparent because it involves a more hidden phenomenon: amid all the social and personal chaos of our world, there are legions of individuals who have found peace and contentment by attempting to follow the kind of life suggested by the Beatitudes, such as being merciful, meek and pure in heart. They aren't the kind of people typically portrayed in our media, though they occasionally get some attention because they stand out in such stark contrast to the norm. When we come across such people and get to know them, we are often stopped in our tracks because they remind us of what might be possible for ourselves, of what was originally intended for us when we were created in God's image.

Among those who have opportunity to observe all kinds of people day in and day out are journalists, and therefore I want to quote one on this issue of life choices:

> My career as a journalist has afforded me opportunities to interview "stars," including NFL football greats, movie actors, music performers,

best-selling authors, politicians, and TV personalities. These are the people who dominate the media. We fawn over them, poring over the minutiae of their lives: the clothes they wear, the food they eat, the aerobic routines they follow, the people they love, the toothpaste they use. Yet I must tell you that, in my limited experience, I have found . . . our "idols" are as miserable a group of people as I have ever met. Most have troubled or broken marriages. Nearly all are incurably dependent on psychotherapy. In a heavy irony, these larger-than-life heroes seem tormented by self-doubt.

I have also spent time with people I call "servants." Doctors and nurses who work among the ultimate outcasts, leprosy patients in rural India, a Princeton graduate who runs a hotel for the homeless in Chicago. Health workers who have left high-paying jobs to serve in a backwater town of Mississippi. Relief workers in Somalia, Sudan, Ethiopia, Bangladesh, and other repositories of human suffering. . . . I was prepared to honor and admire these servants, to hold them up as inspiring examples. I was not prepared to envy them. Yet as I now reflect on the two groups side by side, stars and servants, the servants clearly emerge as the favored ones, the graced ones. Without question, I would rather spend time among the servants than among the stars: they possess qualities of depth and richness and even joy that I have not found elsewhere.[4]

These words could haven written by any honest observer of the human condition. If we are brutally frank, we all know that this observation is on target. In my own case, a series of unexpected events landed me in full-time television instead of parish ministry, and I have spent enough time in both worlds of "stars" and "servants" to learn that public recognition, even adulation, is not enough to guarantee happiness or contentment.

More importantly, when I examine my own heart with ruthless

honesty, I know that I am most content when I have the opportunity to serve others in very individual and personal ways. That is not to say that I don't get satisfaction from doing a good job in my work as a medical journalist—and being recognized for it by my peers and the public—but I have found it more satisfying to help others in ways that no one but the person involved usually ever knows. Based on my own experience, and not just the testimony of others, I am convinced that when Jesus said being a servant is the way to the heart of God, he was telling the truth—not just mouthing platitudes or beatitudes.

But this brings me to the question of reality—as so poignantly penned by my friend: "I just can't do it. I am so far away from meeting that standard that I might as well not even try." That is also the truth: although we may believe that the way of Jesus is the most healthy and whole way of life, we also know that none of us is capable of living that way with any degree of regularity. Where does that leave us?

Obviously, I have no easy answers—meaning answers that are easy to incorporate into our daily lives. And I cringe at television preachers and book writers who suggest that if you "simply" follow Jesus, you will be led to a path of comfort and ease and even financial reward. The truth is that Jesus himself never painted such a rosy picture. In fact, as I read the Gospels, the only gift he promised for sure is that if we attempted to follow his teachings, we would be closer to the heart of God than we would otherwise be—and that he himself would be present in our lives as we attempted to do so.

Now I suspect that this mention of Jesus' "presence in our lives" as a result of our attempt to follow his teachings and example will give some of you spiritual shivers if not outright intellectual indigestion. So let me hasten to add that I am not suggesting that if you attempt to follow Jesus, you can expect mystical magic or emotional ecstasy—though some spiritual sages through the ages have claimed such feelings. But I am saying that I deeply believe that anyone who attempts to follow Jesus—even in tiny footsteps full of failures—will begin a journey of exploration that will lead to a deeper relationship with the God of creation than would otherwise be possible.

So I invite you to begin where the early followers of Jesus began—by following his example, by trying to live the way he did, by putting his teachings into action each day as best you can. As you do, I believe you will be following a path to the heart of God. It is a way of knowing by doing. Ultimately you may discover that what truly matters in life has less to do with getting exactly the right answers than with asking the truly important questions.

EPILOGUE

In my first mini-autobiographical chapter I left out a relatively minor episode that I will now recount—for reasons which will soon become obvious.

When I registered for my junior year at Augustana College in Rock Island, Illinois, I was approached by the debate coach to join the debate team. I told him I had no desire to do so because of the great demands it would place on my time. When he realized he could not talk me into joining, he off-handedly suggested that maybe I could "do oratory" instead. I asked him what that involved, and he replied that all I had to do was write a speech of specified length, memorize it and give it in competition. As a way of assuaging my guilt about saying no to debate, I readily agreed. And without much effort, as I had hoped, I wrote a speech about one of my childhood heroes, Dr. Albert Schweitzer, a German genius (more about him later) who at age thirty had given up a glittering academic and musical career to study medicine so he could go to Africa to minister to the desperate medical needs of that dark continent.

Much to my astonishment—and, I am sure, that of the debate coach—I ended up winning the National Collegiate competition held that year at Michigan State University, a nice moment for me and Augustana. But life went on and I conveniently ignored the example of Albert Schweitzer until recently when one of those "providential moments" I described earlier came along.

Just as I was finishing the final first draft of this manuscript, I was approached by Boston Federal Judge Mark Wolf, a good friend, about helping him with a small project. For many years Mark has been chairman of a wonderful but largely unknown organization called the Albert Schweitzer Fellowship. Based in Boston, its main function is to award about 150 annual mini-fellowships to students in various health professions. The very modest stipends allow these students to engage in a health-care or social project while they continue their studies; the projects, mostly in inner city areas, accomplish great good and often motivate the students to pursue careers in such settings. Mark's request to me was to produce a video that would better explain the work they do—and help raise money for more fellowships.

We have in fact done so as a labor of love—with utterly unexpected consequences for me. As I prepared for work on the video by reading about the life of Albert Schweitzer, I was once again totally captivated by the story of this remarkable man. Schweitzer was born January 14, 1875, in the German province of Alsace. By age thirty he had accomplished more than most of us could imagine doing in several lifetimes. He was an amazingly productive scholar with doctorates in philosophy and theology. He was an ordained minister, a professor at the University of Strasbourg, a concert organist, a world authority on J. S. Bach, a recognized expert on organ building and remodeling, and a prolific writer and author. But then he made a decision that stunned (and in some cases saddened) many of his friends and family: he went to medical school so he could become a doctor and go to Africa to work as a physician. Seven years later he and his new wife, Helene, went to Lambarene in West Africa, where he established a hospital in the jungles along the Ogowe River. For the next fifty-two years, he spent most of his time in that place, helping to build an expanding medical compound that would eventually feed, house and treat an average of one thousand Africans a day! Periodically, he returned to Western civilization to give lectures and organ concerts to raise money for his work in Africa. In 1952 he was awarded the Nobel Peace Prize (in absentia), and he donated the prize money to help build a special hospital for lepers about a half mile from the main hospital grounds. Schweitzer died in Lambarene in 1965 at age ninety. No wonder he inspired so many to attempt lives of service, including a college student in Illinois who wrote a speech about him to get out of doing debate.

But I would not be telling you any of this if it were not for another very complicated and significant aspect of the life of Albert Schweitzer. Throughout his entire life Schweitzer was captivated by the life and teachings of Jesus. With degrees in philosophy and theology he became an ordained minister and before going to Africa, often served part time in church parishes and commonly preached on Sundays. However, he was no ordinary believer. He was in fact a remarkable scholar in the field of studies on "the historical Jesus." At age thirty-one he published the first edition (German, 1906) of what is acknowledged even to this day to be a seminal and remarkable book: *The Quest of the Historical Jesus.* (See "Suggested Reading," where I describe books by and about Schweitzer, including his stimulating autobiography.)

Suffice it to say that Schweitzer's book on Jesus was (and in many ways still is) a theological bombshell. It is far beyond my purpose here to discuss this remarkable book in any detail. But Schweitzer's life in general and this book in particular are very pertinent to my current thinking, because they both speak eloquently to my major thesis: that even in the midst of many difficult intellectual and spiritual questions, it is possible to find enough answers to get on with our spiritual life. And for Schweitzer, as for me, the key to such living—faith in the midst of doubt—was the example set by Jesus.

Put more specifically, Schweitzer's own quest for the historical Jesus did not provide easy answers. But he was able to find in the midst of his many questions and doubts a certainty about what he liked to call the "Spirit of Jesus" that enabled him to give up the possibility of great fame and fortune to pursue a life of service in Africa. He addresses this paradox most poetically in the concluding chapter of his *The Quest of the Historical Jesus*, a chapter titled "Results." Here are a few selections from that chapter—including the famous closing paragraph:

> But the truth is, it is not Jesus as historically known, but Jesus as spiritually arisen within men, who is significant for our time and can help it. Not the historical Jesus, but the spirit which goes forth from him and in the spirits of men strives for new influence and rule, is that which overcomes the world. . . .
>
> Jesus as a concrete historical personality remains a stranger to our time, but His spirit, which lies hidden in His words, is known in simplicity, and its influence is direct. Every saying contains in its own way the whole Jesus. . . .
>
> He comes to us as One unknown, without a name, as of old, by the lake-side, He came to those men who knew Him not. He speaks to us the same word: "Follow thou me!" and sets us to the tasks which He has to

fulfil for our time. He commands. And to those who obey Him, whether they be wise or simple, He will reveal Himself in the toils, the conflicts, the sufferings which they shall pass through in His fellowship, and, as an ineffable mystery, they shall learn in their own experience Who He is.[1]

I am not the only one to disagree with some of Schweitzer's specific conclusions as a theologian and scholar. But it is very difficult to disagree with the huge personal commitment he made as a follower of Jesus. Schweitzer's life stands as an example of the "way of the Lord" in which the heart leads the mind and doing becomes a way of knowing. I have been so profoundly affected by reexamining Schweitzer's life story at this point that I have decided, after my current contract with ABC, to rearrange my life so that I have much more time than I do now to give in direct service to those in need. I don't know how or where that will happen, but I know that for me it must happen if I am to be true to myself and my deep desire to be a follower of Jesus.

SUGGESTED READING

Please regard this section as just one person's recommendations for introductory reading on some of the topics I have addressed. Since *Finding God in the Questions* is not a scholarly book, I am not offering a traditional presentation of sources, though I have attached a bibliography of books referenced by name in the text and notes and in this section. Rather, I am presenting a very limited selection of some of the readings I have found personally helpful in my thinking during the past ten years and while writing this account of my religious journey. I have omitted references to major, primary works of science or theology in favor of books I think are both very readable and in most cases an excellent introduction to further reading that includes primary sources. For the most part these are the kind of books I believe those who have a good high school or college education or who love to read might enjoy—assuming, of course, they have an interest in these topics.

GENERAL SCIENCE

There are dozens of wonderful books on science for the general public—too many for one person to keep up with unless he or she does it for a job or hobby. I will mention three, all written without any overt religious intent. Two are from the exceptional science writer Timothy Ferris. The first is his 1997 book *The Whole Shebang: A State-of-the-Universe(s) Report.* This delightful, mostly understandable survey of modern cosmology is almost as breathtaking as the subject itself, addressing such basic topics as "the shape of space" and the "blast from the past." After the last chapter, Ferris includes a "Contrarian Theological Afterword," in which he shares a personal view of the meaning, if any, of modern cosmology for personal religious belief. As is the rest of the book, it is beautifully written. The second is *Coming of Age in the Milky Way,* first published in 1989 but later reissued as a paperback with a new preface and addendum. These two books together provide a college-level course in modern cosmology.

The other book I recommend for general knowledge is by Bill Bryson, the bestselling author on culture observation and travel. The title *A Short History of Nearly Everything* is an accurate reflection of its content: short and creative but always informative descriptions of just about anything in the natural universe you might want to better understand. In typical Bryson style the book is eminently readable and full of humor, but it may also be the best general introduction available (as of the summer of 2003) to natural science for the non-scientific person.

Science from a Religious Perspective

The following recommended books clearly are written with a religious bias, but they are also informative and creatively intelligent. I begin by trumpeting the writings of John Polkinghorne, who is both a former Cambridge (England) professor of mathematical physics and a current Anglican priest. His writings are at once delightful and serious, and I have yet to read anything by him that was not worth the time. You will find dozens of short and longer works from his prolific pen. To start with, I recommend his slim 1996 volume *Quarks, Chaos and Christianity: Questions to Science and Religion.* It is not at all a narrow-minded defense of the Christian religion but a spirited and provocative defense of the possibility, even desirability, of being both scientific and spiritual. As the next step I suggest his *Science & Theology: An Introduction.*

Another delightful author, also a physicist but unlike Polkinghorne not formally religious, is Paul Davies. He too has written many books, but the one I have most enjoyed is his 1983 volume, *God and the New Physics.* He is an easy yet provocative read.

A much more dense and difficult book is Michael J. Denton's *Nature's Destiny: How the Laws of Biology Reveal Purpose in the Universe.* As the title indicates, Denton focuses on the world of biology and biochemistry as a source of evidence for intelligent design. (You may recall that I quoted him extensively in part one of this book.) Denton has both an M.D. and a Ph.D. in developmental biology. This is not an easy book to read, but it's well worth the time.

I also invite you to consider a book that blends lay science and popular theology, written by a very bright man with a Ph.D. in philosophy from Harvard. Patrick Glynn's 1997 book *God: The Evidence* argues for the existence of God from several traditional viewpoints but with very modern twists. He is a fine writer and also entertaining in the best sense of that word. Although I do not agree with all his points, I find his overall argument quite compelling. And for those of you interested in a modern look at the possible connections be-

tween religious faith and health, I would recommend Harold
Koenig's *The Healing Power of Faith.*

INTELLIGENT DESIGN

The label *intelligent design* identifies a movement supporting the
concept that intelligence and intentional design underlie the origins
of our universe. The "ID" movement is a strange mixture of tributar-
ies from the religious right to the spiritual left and almost everything
in between. It is far beyond my scope to indicate the complexity of this
movement—and its detractors' criticisms—but for an overall picture
of this vibrant debate I would encourage you to start with the 2001
book *Intelligent Design Creationism and Its Critics,* edited by Robert
T. Pennock. You will notice the word *creationism* in the title, suggesting that this volume is tilted toward the critics of intelligent design
who often see it as little more that a cover for old-fashioned creationist
arguments from religious fundamentalists. However, there is a genu-
inely spirited and usually respectful dialogue contained in the back-
and-forth format of essays selected for this volume—and it is a good
place to begin to get the flavor of the currently vigorous debate provoked by modern proponents of intelligent design. For further reading
directly from the leading proponents of the ID movement I suggest
Darwin's Black Box by Michael Behe, *The Creation Hypothesis* edited
by J. P. Moreland, *Signs of Intelligence* edited by William Dembski
and James Kushiner, and *The Design Revolution* by William Dembski.
These books will lead you to many more of similar bent.

Finally, I recommend the older classics of C. S. Lewis and Blaise
Pascal. Lewis was a highly respected English literature scholar who
taught at both Oxford and Cambridge in the middle part of the twen-

tieth century. However, today he is more widely known as the prolific writer of Christian apologetics—that is, books attempting to rationally support the claims of the Christian religion. Anything written by Lewis is worth reading for its literate and often lyrical style, but the one book most often recommended is the compilation of three talks first given on the radio in Britain in the early 1940s and published later under the title *Mere Christianity.* (Lewis is also well known for his children's books, especially *The Lion, the Witch, and the Wardrobe,* the first of eight books in the Chronicles of Narnia series, and his fantasy trilogy *Out of the Silent Planet, Perelandra* and *That Hideous Strength.)*

Blaise Pascal was a brilliant seventeenth-century French scientist and mathematician who also wrote a series of reflections *(pensées)* before his tragically premature death at age thirty-nine. I recommend a particular edition of them edited, outlined and explained by Peter Kreeft and titled *Christianity for Modern Pagans.*

THE BIBLE

I wouldn't even begin to consider recommending a particular translation of the Bible. But I will, as promised, suggest a particular version of a New Testament "harmony"—a book that puts the similar passages from the four Gospels side by side—*A Harmony of the Four Gospels* by Orville Daniel, which uses the New International Version.

For a popularized and nonscholarly look at the history of the Bible, I suggest Kenneth Davis's *Don't Know Much About the Bible,* part of his popular series with the same title formats. For much more scholarly but accessible information about the Bible, I recommend *The Oxford Companion to the Bible,* edited by Bruce Metzger and

Michael Coogan. This volume contains brief but very informative essays about almost any subject related to the content and history of the Bible. (*The Oxford Companion to Christian Thought* is a similarly invaluable resource for information on the history and thought of the Christian religion.)

For a more specific look at the world of the Hebrew Scriptures and its influence on Jesus and Christianity, I suggest two books. Thomas Cahill's *The Gifts of the Jews* is a poetic and mystical look at the history of Judaism. Marvin Wilson's *Our Father Abraham* looks more specifically at the early relations between Jews and Christians and the subsequent troubled history between them. (I also heartily recommend Cahill's companion book on the New Testament, *Desire of the Everlasting Hills.*)

THE LIFE AND TEACHINGS OF JESUS

It is truly impossible to recommend selected reading that does full justice to the wide range of views on the life and teachings of Jesus. However, I recommend one relatively recent book (2001) that can serve as a kind of reference to and summary of the vast literature written about Jesus. Clinton Bennett is a Baptist minister and former missionary who is also a fine scholar and student of world religions. His *In Search of Jesus: Insider and Outsider Images* is an amazing compilation of the many attempts to capture the story of Jesus by both insiders (those who claim to be Christians) and outsiders (those from other religious traditions). You can look up almost any writer on the subject of Jesus and find a brief but fair summary of that person's writings and point of view. It is a great one-stop source of quick summary information.

Beyond that primary recommendation, if I were forced to pick just one book that provides a very readable introduction to two very different ways of thinking about "the historical Jesus" it would be *The Meaning of Jesus: Two Visions* by Marcus Borg and N. T. Wright. Both are first-rate scholars who know and respect each other but who come to very different conclusions about what historical research can conclude about Jesus. They write back and forth in response to each other about such basic issues as the Gospel sources, the crucifixion, the resurrection and the divinity of Jesus. The book may leave your head and heart spinning, but it will give you an honest introduction into the wide world of modern Jesus scholarship. You can then pursue the many other writings from both authors as you wish.

I have personally concluded that the approach taken by N. T. Wright to Jesus studies is a balanced and centrist path. Therefore I recommend anything from this prolific writer, but for quick insight into his approach and conclusions I call attention to two very short books of his: *Who Was Jesus?* (1992, only 103 pages) and *The Challenge of Jesus* (1999, a slightly longer 197 pages) summarize much of his approach. He is also engaged in a massive six-part series (*Christian Origins and the Question of God*), of which three books have been published to date: *The New Testament and the People of God* (1992), *Jesus and the Victory of God* (1996) and *The Resurrection of the Son of God* (2003). This last volume is a monumental examination of past and current thinking about the resurrection (including a detailed examination of the biblical accounts) with a spirited defense of Jesus' bodily resurrection.

There are many other scholars worthy of mention, such as E. P.

Sanders, John P. Meier, John Dominic Crossan, Ben Witherington III and Raymond E. Brown—to name just a few. However, I want to mention the works of a writer who would, I assume, never claim to be a scholar but who has certainly done his homework. Philip Yancey is probably the best-known and bestselling author among more conservative Christian circles. However, for good reason, he also has a wide audience outside such circles. He has a unique manner of taking large amounts of often complicated and controversial information and putting it into stimulating and comprehensible form. His use of real-life examples, often from his own personal religious pilgrimage, make difficult ideas digestible. I recommend any of his books, but perhaps the one most pertinent to the issues I have discussed in this book is *The Jesus I Never Knew.* I also heartily recommend his book *Rumors of Another World,* which explores the strange juxtaposition of the intermingling of the material and spiritual so many of us experience in our daily lives. (For those specifically interested in the question of unwarranted suffering, I recommend Yancey's *Where Is God When It Hurts?* along with C. S. Lewis's *The Problem of Pain* and Harold Kushner's *When Bad Things Happen to Good People.*)

Finally, for those whose interest in Albert Schweitzer has been aroused by my epilogue, I recommend starting with his wonderful autobiography, *Out of My Life and Thought.* The most definitive biography of Schweitzer is probably James Brabazon's *Albert Schweitzer: A Biography.* And for those with the appetite for controversial biblical scholarship, his *The Quest of the Historical Jesus* is still regarded as a classic now almost a century since it was first published.

Notes

Chapter 2: Is the Universe an Accident?

[1]Thomas Hardy, *Far from the Madding Crowd* (1912; reprint, New York: Modern Library, 2001), pp. 8-9.

[2]Chet Raymo, *Boston Globe*, January 17, 2000.

[3]Timothy Ferris, *The Whole Shebang* (New York: Simon & Schuster, 1997), pp. 149-50.

[4]Timothy Ferris, *Coming of Age in the Mily Way* (New York: Morrow, 1988), p. 288.

[5]Bill Bryson, *A Short History of Nearly Everything* (New York: Broadway Books, 2003), p. 145.

[6]Niels Bohr, quoted in Ferris, *Coming of Age in the Milky Way*, p. 266.

[7]Actually, the latest wrinkle in cosmology and physics is so-called string theory, which sees the universe as eleven dimensions of infinitesimal "strings" of energy. This concept is way beyond the scope of this book, but you will find a more than adequate introduction in Ferris's *The Whole Shebang*, pp. 220-28. According to the October 26, 2003, *New York Times* (sec. 8, p. 12) Edward Witten, one of the leading expositors of this theory, describes the strange nature of his M theory component of string theory (the M stands for "membranes") by saying, "M stands for magic, mystery or matrix, according to taste. Some cynics have also occasionally suggested that M may also stand for murky, because our level of understanding of the theory is so primitive."

[8]Patrick Glynn, *God: The Evidence: The Reconciliation of Faith and Reason in a Postsecular World* (Rocklin, Calif.: Forum, 1997).

[9]Ibid., pp. 44-45.

[10]Fred Hoyle, quoted in "Hoyle on Evolution," *Nature*, November, 12, 1981, p. 105.

[11]Charles Darwin, *Origin of Species*, 6th ed. (New York: New York University Press, 1988), p. 154.

[12]John Polkinghorne, *Quarks, Chaos & Christianity* (New York: Crossroad, 1996), p. 40, italics added.

Chapter 3: How Did We Get Here?

[1]Michael Denton, *Nature's Destiny* (New York: Free Press, 1998), p. 11.

[2]Cited in Michael J. Murray, ed., *Reason for the Hope Within* (Grand Rapids: Eerdmans, 1999), p. 49.

[3]Patrick Glynn, *God: the Evidence: The Reconciliation of Faith and Reason in a Postsecular World* (Rocklin, Calif.: Forum, 1997), p. 29.

[4]Paul Davies, *God and the New Physics* (New York: Simon & Schuster, 1983), p. 189.

[5]I strongly urge you to read Denton's *Nature's Destiny* in its entirety.

[6]Denton, *Nature's Destiny*, p. 153.

[7]Ibid., p. 154.

[8]Ibid., p. 172.

[9]Carter's paper is titled "Large Number Coincidences and the Anthropic Principle in Cosmology."

[10]John Polkinghorne, *Quarks, Chaos & Christianity* (New York: Crossroad, 1996), pp. 24-25.

[11]Peter Kreeft, *Christianity for Modern Pagans* (San Francisco: Ignatius Press, 1993), p. 245.

[12]Woody Allen, quoted in *The Creation Hypothesis*, ed. J. P. Moreland (Downers Grove, Ill.: InterVarsity Press, 1994), p. 116.

[13]Norwood Russell Hanson, quoted in ibid., p. 117.

[14]Blaise Pascal, quoted in Kreeft, *Christianity for Modern Pagans*, p. 247.

[15]Ibid., p. 213.

[16]Barbara Brown Taylor, "Physics and Faith: The Luminous Web," *Christian Century*, June 2-9, 1999, pp. 617-18.

Chapter 4: Who Are We?

[1]This famous quote comes from the conclusion of Kant's major work, *The Critique of Pure Reason*. You will find slight variations of the quote depending on specific translations.

[2]Randy Thornhill and Craig T. Palmer, *The Natural History of Rape: Biological Bases of Sexual Coercion* (Cambridge, Mass.: MIT Press, 2000).

[3]Rudolf Otto, *The Idea of the Holy*, trans. John W. Harvey (New York: Oxford University Press, 1958), p. 22.

[4]Andrew Newberg, Eugene D'Aquili and Vince Rause, *Why God Won't Go Away: Brain Science and the Biology of Belief* (New York: Ballantine, 2001), p. 143.

[5]From a special report by the Commission on Children at Risk, "Hardwired to Connect: The New Scientific Case for Authoritative Communities" (New York: Institute for American Values, 2003), pp. 6, 7, 15, 29.

[6]Private correspondence; used by permission.

Chapter 5: Why Bother with Religion and the Bible?

[1]Thomas Cahill, *The Gifts of the Jews* (New York: Doubleday, 1998), pp. 239-40.

[2]Luke Timothy Johnson, *The Real Jesus* (New York: HarperCollins, 1996), p. 114.

[3]See N. T. Wright, *The New Testament and the People of God* (Minneapolis: Fortress, 1992), pp. 422-24.

[4]Thomas Cahill, *Desire of the Everlasting Hills* (New York: Doubleday, 1999), pp. 283-85.

[5]For a scholarly but lively assessment of these sources I recommend you read Philip Jenkins, *Hidden Gospels: How the Search for Jesus Lost Its Way* (Cambridge: Oxford University Press, 2001).

Chapter 6: What Did Jesus Teach?

[1]M. Scott Peck, *Further Along the Road Less Traveled* (New York: Simon & Schuster, 1993), pp. 160-61.

[2]Robert McAfee Brown, *The Bible Speaks to You* (Louisville, Ky.: Westminster John Knox, 1955), p. 21.

Chapter 7: Who Was Jesus?

[1]M. Scott Peck, *People of the Lie* (New York: Simon & Schuster, 1983), pp. 268-69.

[2]Stephen Ulstein, *Growing Up Fundamentalist* (Downers Grove, Ill.: InterVarsity Press, 1995), pp. 27-28.

[3]John Irving, *A Prayer for Owen Meany* (New York: Ballantine, 1989), p. 278.

[4]Thomas Cahill, *Desire of the Everlasting Hills* (New York: Doubleday, 1999), pp. 273-75.

[5]Williston Walker, *A History of the Christian Church* (New York: Charles Scribner's Sons, 1959).

[6]For a stunning account of the years in which the followers of Jesus went from being often persecuted to being the official religion of the Roman Empire, see Richard Rubenstein's *When Jesus Became God: The Epic Fight over Christ's Divinity in the Last Days of Rome* (New York: Harcourt Brace, 1999).

[7]Personal correspondence, used by permission.

[8]N. T. Wright, *The Original Jesus* (Grand Rapids: Eerdmans, 1996), pp. 78-79.

Chapter 8: How Should Faith Shape Our Lives?

[1]Philip Yancey, *The Jesus I Never Knew* (Grand Rapids: Zondervan, 1995), p. 109.

[2]Ibid., p. 130.

[3]J. B. Phillips, quoted in Yancey, *Jesus I Never Knew*, p. 113.

[4]M. Scott Peck, *Further Along the Road Less Traveled* (New York: Simon & Schuster, 1993), p. 181.

Chapter 9: Is God in Control?

[1]On a sad note, I must report the death at age 77 of the wonderfully prophetic Dr. Anderson.

[2]C. S. Lewis, *The Great Divorce* (New York: Macmillan, 1957), p. 69.

[3]George McGovern, in *The Nation*, April 21, 2003.

[4]From a private conversation, used by permission.

[5]Blaise Pascal, quoted in Peter Kreeft, *Christianity for Modern Pagans* (San Francisco: Ignatius Press, 1993), p. 294, italics added.

Chapter 10: Can We Bet on the Heart of God?

[1]Attributed broadly to Franz Kafka. See <www.freedomsnest.com>.

[2]Dorothy Day, "Room for Christ," *The Catholic Worker*, December 1945, p. 2.

[3]Spoken of Dorothy Day in March 1972, when she was awarded the Laetare Medal, the University of Notre Dame's highest honor.

[4]Philip Yancey, *The Jesus I Never Knew* (Grand Rapids: Zondervan, 1995), p. 117.

Epilogue

[1]Albert Schweitzer, *The Quest of the Historical Jesus* (Baltimore: Johns Hopkins University Press, 1998), pp. 401, 403.

BIBLIOGRAPHY

Behe, Michael, J. *Darwin's Black Box: The Biochemical Challenge to Evolution*. New York: Simon & Schuster, 1996.

Bennett, Clinton. *In Search of Jesus: Insider and Outsider Images*. New York: Continuum, 2001.

Borg, Marcus J., and N. T. Wright. *The Meaning of Jesus: Two Visions*. New York: HarperCollins, 1999.

Brabazon, James. *Albert Schweitzer: A Biography*, 2nd ed. Syracuse: Syracuse University Press, 2000.

Brown, Robert McAfee. *The Bible Speaks to You*. Philadelphia: Westminster Press, 1995.

Bryson, Bill. *A Short History of Nearly Everything*. New York: Broadway Books, 2003.

Cahill, Thomas. *Desire of the Everlasting Hills: The World Before and After Jesus*. New York: Doubleday, 1999.

———. *The Gifts of the Jews: How a Tribe of Desert Nomads Changed the Way Everyone Thinks and Feels*. New York: Doubleday, 1998.

Daniel, Orville E. *A Harmony of the Four Gospels: The New International Version*, 2nd ed. Grand Rapids: Baker, 1996.

Darwin, Charles. *The Origin of Species*. New York: Gramercy Books, 1979.

Davies, Paul. *God & The New Physics*. New York: Simon & Schuster, 1983.

Davis, Kenneth C. *Don't Know Much About the Bible: Everything You Need to Know About the Good Book but Never Learned*. New York: William Morrow, 1998.

Dembski, William A. *The Design Revolution: Answering the Toughest Questions About Intelligent Design.* Downers Grove, Ill.: InterVarsity Press, 2004.

Dembski, William A., and James M. Kushiner, eds. *Signs of Intelligence: Understanding Intelligent Design.* Grand Rapids: Brazos, 2001.

Denton, Michael J. *Nature's Destiny: How the Laws of Biology Reveal Purpose in the Universe.* New York: Free Press, 1998.

Ferris, Timothy. *Coming of Age in the Milky Way.* New York: Perennial, 2003.

———. *The Whole Shebang: A State-of-the-Universe(s) Report.* New York: Simon & Schuster, 1997.

Glynn, Patrick. *God: The Evidence: The Reconciliation of Faith and Reason in a Postsecular World.* Rocklin, Calif.: Forum, 1997.

Hardy, Thomas. *Far from the Madding Crowd.* Rev. ed. (New York: Modern Library, 1998).

Hastings, Adrian, Alister Mason, and Hugh Pyper, eds. *The Oxford Companion to Christian Thought.* New York: Oxford University Press, 2000.

Jenkins, Philip. *Hidden Gospels: How the Search for Jesus Lost Its Way.* Cambridge: Oxford University Press, 2001.

Johnson, Luke Timothy. *The Real Jesus: The Misguided Quest for the Historical Jesus and the Truth of the Traditional Gospels.* New York: HarperCollins, 1996.

Koenig, Harold G. *The Healing Power of Faith: Science Explores Medicine's Last Great Frontier.* New York: Simon & Schuster, 1999.

Kreeft, Peter. *Christianity for Modern Pagans: Pascal's Pensees Edited, Outlined and Explained.* San Francisco: Ignatius Press, 1993.

Kushner, Harold S. *When Bad Things Happen to Good People.* New York: Schocken, 1981.

Lewis, C. S. *The Great Divorce.* New York: Macmillan, 1957.

———. *Mere Christianity.* Westwood, N.J.: Barbour, n.d.

———. *The Problem of Pain.* New York: Macmillan, 1959.

Metzger, Bruce M., and Michael D. Coogan, eds. *The Oxford Companion to the Bible.* New York: Oxford University Press, 1993.

Moreland, J. P., ed. *The Creation Hypothesis: Scientific Evidence for an Intelligent Designer.* Downers Grove, Ill.: InterVarsity Press, 1994.

Newberg, Andrew, Eugene D'Aquili, and Vince Rause. *Why God Won't Go Away: Brain Science and the Biology of Belief.* New York: Ballantine, 2001.

Otto, Rudolf. *The Idea of the Holy*, trans. John W. Harvey. New York: Oxford University Press, 1958.

Peck, M. Scott. *Further Along the Road Less Traveled.* New York: Simon & Schuster, 1993.

——. *People of the Lie: The Hope for Healing Human Evil.* New York: Simon & Schuster, 1983.

——. *The Road Less Traveled: A New Psychology of Love, Traditional Values and Spiritual Growth.* New York: Simon & Schuster, 1978.

——. *The Road Less Traveled and Beyond: Spiritual Growth in an Age of Anxiety.* New York: Simon & Schuster, 1997.

Pennock, Robert T., ed. *Intelligent Design Creationism and Its Critics: Philosophical, Theological, and Scientific Perspectives.* Cambridge, Mass.: MIT Press, 2001.

Polkinghorne, John. *Quarks, Chaos & Christianity: Questions to Science and Religion.* New York: Crossroad, 1996.

——. *Science and Theology: An Introduction.* Minneapolis: Fortress Press, 1998.

Rubenstein, Richard E. *When Jesus Became God: The Epic Fight over Christ's Divinity in the Last Days of Rome.* New York: Harcourt Brace, 1999.

Schweitzer, Albert. *Out of My Life and Thought.* Baltimore: The Johns Hopkins University Press, 1998.

——. *The Quest of the Historical Jesus.* Baltimore: The Johns Hopkins University Press, 1998.

Ulstein, Stephen. *Growing Up Fundamentalist.* Downers Grove, Ill.: Inter-
    Varsity Press, 1995.

Walker, Williston. *A History of the Christian Church.* New York: Charles
    Scribner's Sons, 1959.

Wilson, Marvin R. *Our Father Abraham: Jewish Roots of the Christian
    Faith.* Grand Rapids: Eerdmans, 1989.

Wright, N. T. *The Challenge of Jesus: Rediscovering Who Jesus Was and Is.*
    Downers Grove, Ill.: InterVarsity Press, 1999.

——. *Jesus and the Victory of God.* Minneapolis: Fortress, 1996.

——. *The New Testament and the People of God.* Minneapolis: Fortress,
    1992.

——. *The Original Jesus.* Grand Rapids: Eerdmans, 1996.

——. *The Resurrection of the Son of God.* Minneapolis: Fortress, 2003.

——. *Who Was Jesus?* Grand Rapids: Eerdmans, 1992.

Yancey, Philip. *The Jesus I Never Knew.* Grand Rapids: Zondervan, 1995.

——. *Rumors of Another World.* Grand Rapids: Zondervan, 2003.

——. *Where Is God When It Hurts?* Grand Rapids: Zondervan, 1990.